The Healing Wisdom of the Forest

Timeless Lessons of Renewal, Tranquility, and Joy

Anthony D. Fredericks

Health Communications, Inc.
Mt. Pleasant, SC
www.hcibooks.com

Library of Congress Cataloging-in-Publication Data
is available through the Library of Congress

ISBN-13: 978-0-7573-2537-3 (Paperback)
ISBN-10: 0-7573-2537-8 (Paperback)
ISBN-13: 978-0-7573-2538-0 (ePub)
ISBN-10: 0-7573-2538-6 (ePub)

Publisher: Health Communications, Inc.
1240 Winnowing Way, Suite 102
Mt. Pleasant, SC 29466

Cover illustration by Rebecca Noelle Purvis (https://rebeccanoelleartstudio.com)
Cover, interior design, and formatting by Larissa Hise Henoch

For Beverly,
who, like trees in a forest,
always reaches for the sun

Selected Books by Anthony D. Fredericks

ADULT NONFICTION

In Search of the Old Ones: An Odyssey among Ancient Trees

Two-Minute Habits: Small Habits, Dynamic Creativity

Horseshoe Crab: Biography of a Survivor

Writing Children's Books: Everything You Need to Know from Story Creation to Getting Published

Desert Dinosaurs: Discovering Prehistoric Sites in the American Southwest

From Fizzle to Sizzle: The Hidden Forces Crushing Your Creativity and How You Can Overcome Them

The Secret Life of Clams: The Mysteries and Magic of Our Favorite Shellfish

The Adjunct Professor's Complete Guide to Teaching College (2nd Ed.): How to Be an Effective and Successful Instructor

Walking with Dinosaurs: Rediscovering Colorado's Prehistoric Beasts

Ace Your Teacher Interview (3rd Ed.): 158 Fantastic Answers to Tough Interview Questions

CHILDREN'S BOOKS

Tall Tall Tree

I Am the Desert

Under One Rock: Bugs, Slugs and Other Ughs

The Tsunami Quilt: Grandfather's Story

A is for Anaconda: A Rainforest Alphabet

Desert Night, Desert Day

Around One Log: Chipmunks, Spiders, and Creepy Insiders

Near One Cattail: Turtles, Logs and Leaping Frogs

Mountain Night, Mountain Day

P is for Prairie Dog: A Prairie Alphabet

In One Tidepool: Crabs, Snails and Salty Tails

Moose

Contents

Preface

You fill up my senses
like a night in the forest.
—JOHN DENVER

It was a crystalline dusk; faint stars speckled a darkening sky. They peeked through branches and wrapped around edges of the forest—silent harbingers of an approaching night deep in the High Sierra Mountains.

I stood on the margin of Grassy Lake (aka Jackson Lake), an expanse of shadowed waters, a bouldered shoreline, and the rich ecology of ancient mountains. I was nine years old, and my father and I were camped in this serenity for two weeks of fly-fishing in unclouded streams. Days hiking alpine trails, napping in the company of curious chipmunks and persistent mosquitoes, and the experience of fresh-caught golden trout fried in a cast-iron pan and served on tin plates beneath an assembly of trees were also part of this annual pilgrimage. These ventures began when I was seven and continued through my teens.

They have never left my consciousness.

Each August, my father and I would pack up the Buick with sleeping bags, fishing gear, and the indispensable Coleman Stove, and journey north out of Los Angeles on Highway 14. We would drive across the simmer of the inland desert and quickly slip through the outposts of Palmdale, Lancaster, and Mojave. At Walker Pass we would turn north onto Route 395 and begin our ascent into the ancient geography of eastern California. This part of the journey took us through the rustic towns of Little Lake, Olancha, Lone Pine, Independence, Big Pine, and Bishop. A long day of asphalt highways and hardscrabble landscapes would eventually deposit us in Mammoth Lakes. We would take a cabin for the night, and early the next morning, cupping cardboard cups of hot chocolate and dark coffee, we would check in at the Mammoth Lakes Pack Outfit.

There, we would transport our supplies to a waiting line of pack horses—solid stock that traversed mountain trails with resolution and patience. Necessary camping supplies and food were tucked into canvas bags and loaded side to side on several hooved transports. Cowboy hats canted to the side, we would mount our horses, and in the company of a practiced (and often loquacious) wrangler, we would begin the nine-hour journey deep into the John Muir Wilderness. Hour after hour we passed an embrace of escarpments, orbited azure lakes, and climbed looping switchbacks etched upon a rocky landscape. Occasionally, we would pause beside a stream to water the horses or unwater ourselves. A late afternoon sun eventually brought us to Grassy Lake, an expanse of frigid water set amid towering evergreens and a carpet of meadow at 9,600 feet. Coursing through these mountains were varied mountain streams that would soon experience Parachute Adams, Sparkle Duns, Pheasant Tails, and other trout flies gently laid upon their ripples.

On one particular twilight, I stood beside the shore surrounded by silence. No planes overhead, no artificial soundtracks, and not a whisper of human existence for miles around. The stillness was persistent; the quiet ethereal. Even the insects had taken respite. A light wind, pregnant with pine, brushed by my face, encircled granite boulders, and drifted through the web of branches and snags behind.

Then, like tiny dancers on an oversized stage, I saw them. A doe and her fawn meandered out of the virgin forest to the banks of an unhurried stream. They hesitated, as do all ungulates when moving from one ecosystem to another. I knew they were not halted on my behalf. Humans were an anomaly in this wilderness, and I was certain they could scarcely find me standing in the shadows on the opposite shore. They were patient, nonetheless, stopping occasionally to nibble a few clusters of grass in their prenocturnal waltz.

Each one dipped its head to the water and took a long drink. Both heads eventually raised, and they nuzzled each other for brief moments. Then they turned their silhouettes to the rising moon and ambled back to the comfort of thick trees. The vision lasted but a scant five minutes, yet its details are forever on my conscience as though an anniversary or a grandchild's birth date.

The deer had been secured by the sanctuary of the forest—both before and after their passage. The trees were both home and refuge. The two had slipped from the forest's embrace to refresh themselves and then, just as silently, crept back to its abiding shelter. Why was the forest so critical? Did it have secrets known only to deer and other animals, secrets long concealed from human experience? Does living in a forest or walking through its trees give one brave insights or consequential comfort against an outside world with the possibility of danger? Did the doe and her fawn know something about an arboreal environment unfelt by a preadolescent boy? I felt a message, but I was naïve and unaware of how to search or even what to look for.

A brief moment in 1956 was sufficient to spark a lifelong quest for evergreen truths harbored by groves, orchards, and long expanses of powerful timbers. Now, as someone well ensconced in his eighth decade, I have considered determination to examine the uncommon wisdom of trees, and the persistent lessons cached among their branches.

I have learned much.

Introduction

Going to the woods is going home, for I suppose we came from the woods originally.

—JOHN MUIR

As a wise philosopher once noted, "Life is tough!" Consequently, we frequently react (negatively) to daily inconveniences, we wrestle with unnecessary stressors to our day, and we become immobilized by injustices and the seeming unfairness of daily living.

Too often, we lose sight of the big picture. We think less of others and less of ourselves. Life becomes a constant battle of trying to endure one challenging event after another and seems to be a series of nonstop emergencies. We move from one crisis to another. Many times, we spend so much time and energy trying to quell our issues that we fail to prevent them in the first place. We become more reactive and less proactive. It is as though we are caught in a personal whirlpool from which there is little escape.

Yeah, life is tough!

Many years ago, while pursuing my master's degree, I enrolled in an advanced psychology class. Early in the course, our instructor invited us to participate in an activity that has never left me. He asked each of us to bring in one three-by-five-inch index card to the next class with our names hand-lettered on the front in large letters. We were also instructed to rule the back of our individual card into sixty half-inch squares.

During the subsequent class, the instructor gave us an unusual set of instructions. First, he directed us to carry the cards with us everywhere throughout the upcoming week. Then he told us that each time someone said something negative to us we were to tear out one of the squares on the card and discard it. If someone gave us a task to do that we didn't choose to do, we were to tear out a square. If someone didn't smile at us when we smiled at them in the supermarket or cafeteria line, we were to tear out a square. If someone said an unkind word or failed to give us a compliment, we were to tear out a square. We were instructed to bring what was left of the cards to class the following week.

During the next class, we all sat in a circle and shared our experiences. Our instructor informed us that the cards represented the amount of control each of us has over the slights and injustices of our daily lives. In other words, each tear off was a way of letting go of a problem or negative situation.

The instructor made the point that each of us had command over the shape of our lives. If someone did something we didn't like or said something inappropriate, we had the power to excise that event from our lives. Although we were all dealt a different set of cards, it was what we each did with our respective cards that was important. Most significant was that we could hang on to the frustrations of our daily lives or we could take charge and remove them.

Happily, there are ways we can ease our burdens and bring more harmony into our lives. It's a change in perspective—a fresh and vibrant way of reminding us what is important and what is necessary in a peaceful life. Its prophets are all around—to be found in your backyard, an urban botanical garden, a state forest, or a sprawling assembly of timbers in a national park. Their "lessons" are visionary and eternal. Not only will they influence your mind; so, too, will they touch your soul. Their instruction is life-affirming and long-lasting.

As with that lesson of mine long ago, you will also come to understand that we each have the option to choose a wholesome, enjoyable purpose that significantly reduces the stress in our daily lives, positively influences our outlook and production, contributes to a healthier lifestyle, makes us more productive as human beings, and solves a myriad of everyday problems. Much of that orientation involves a communion, or re-communion, with nature—a return to our roots. It is a reawakening of our inner core and an embrace of a world with subtle lessons and patient insights. Or as noted naturalist E. O. Wilson once said, "Nature holds the key to our aesthetic, intellectual, cognitive, and even spiritual satisfaction."

Trees offer a unique comprehension of life. They are, in so many ways, exemplars of determination and vibrancy, persistence and growth. Many authors, along with a cadre of researchers, have celebrated our natural connection to nature. Yet observers have also lamented the fact that in our busy and crowded lives we have lost touch with that world—not only a world of wonder, but one of insight and explanation.

In answer, this book underscores nature as a great healer, but only if you take time to experience it firsthand. As our ancestors knew, you can learn much in the company of trees. More specifically, you can enjoy a compendium of practical advice that will change your life for the better; a collection of scientific and psychological insights that can renew and reinvigorate; a game plan, if you will, that will alter habits and improve your outlook.

For the long term.

This book welcomes forests as fonts of knowledge, beacons of enlightenment, and exemplars of inner peace and satisfaction. Here is a way to take back control of who you are and what you can become—a way to improve your personal "index card." What you will discover is that trees are teachers of the highest order. Wide and fertile forests, sprawling orchards, ancient woodlands, and towering woods allow you to stand back and take a look at the larger picture. You'll discover powerful ideas to help you refocus and relax. You'll learn strategies to reinvigorate your life. You'll reduce everyday stressors and frustrations with positivity and resolve. Most importantly, you'll read about techniques that help bring out more of the best in yourself.

Know that the wisdom of trees is forever writ.

They await your attention.

Part I

Branch Out

Always Leave a Campsite Better . . .

Be as useful as a tree! Give life to others;
be shelter to everyone; grant fruits to all!
Be good like a tree!
—MEHMET MURAT ILDAN

As you may recall from the preface, in the 1950s and early 1960s, my father and I spent two weeks every summer camping deep in the John Muir Wilderness of the Sierra Nevada Mountains. Each day we would set out from our campsite, hiking to various lakes, through acres of undisturbed woods, along winding streams, and past verdant meadows. Our goal: to fish for rainbow and golden trout across this unspoiled wilderness.

During those fishing trips my father taught me one of life's most important lessons. For thirteen days we would fish every day. But on the fourteenth day, we would stay in camp to clean up, repair a wooden table, clear out a part of the trail, strengthen a lean-to, gather errant bits of litter, and other such tasks. As my father would frequently tell me, "Always leave a campsite better than you found it." And we did.

That maxim has stayed with me for long years. That embrace may be one of the reasons why I became an educator. I always sought to make students' lives better—to strengthen their self-concepts, to repair any injustices, and to build a healthy regard for learning. When I became a teacher trainer, I wanted my undergraduate students (all future classroom teachers) to pass that baton along.

Always leave students better than you found them.

The saying also rings true in other aspects of our lives—in our interactions with family members, colleagues, and even the strangers we meet every day. When we approach others with the question "How can I make this person's life a little better than I found it?," we are filled with a limitless sense of direction and purpose. The question motivates us to make a positive change in someone's day—a change for the better.

Simply waking up each day to thoughts of how we might improve the lives of those with whom we live, work, and interact, we achieve a heightened level of personal satisfaction in our own lives. Strengthening the lives of others is the truest form of compassion, the epitome of humanity.

A friend recently shared photographs and a video of several stately ponderosa pines well established around her northern California home. They reminded me of my childhood ventures through long expanses of these trees—a species common across western states. In my admiration, I was also reminded that ponderosas significantly enrich the lives of others.

Many types of wildlife rely on ponderosas for their food. Squirrels gather ponderosa pine seeds as food. Several types of birds, such as sapsuckers, drill horizontal holes in ponderosas to get at the sap—an important food source. Insects that typically gather on these pines are also necessary for a variety of birds. Mammals, such as elk and mule deer, typically use these trees for shelter.

The lives of humans have also been enriched by these iconic trees. Ponderosa pines supply timber for building, firewood for comfort, and medicines for various ailments. Native Americans used the inner bark as food in times of starvation and as a form of chewing gum. The tree's resin was used as a salve for skin problems and to soothe achy joints.

Ponderosas make the lives of others (humans and animals) a little better.

Reaching out and sharing a compliment or extending a helping hand is kindness at its best. Far too many of us go through life without ever receiving a thoughtful word or heartfelt appreciation. We are often so caught up in our own challenges and issues that we forget that others experience challenges, too. Making their day—or their life—a little better than you found it always has a positive impact. Orienting your life to giving enriches the lives of others. It puts a smile on their soul. And yours, too!

In my research for this book, I picked up a great quote: "Kinda cool to think someone somewhere is having the best day of their life today." To that let's add, "Kinda cool to think that you might help make that happen."

In Practice:

Doing good for others doesn't have to involve big events or grand gestures. Small everyday behaviors send a positive message, too. A generous smile, a friendly comment, a sincere handshake, a welcoming greeting, a bouquet of flowers, a written note, a complimentary treat, an unexpected compliment, being a good listener, holding a door open, comforting someone, running an errand, an invitation to help, an engaging laugh, and a warm "Hello" are things we can do every day. They are gifts from the heart rather than obligations from the mind. The simple act of reaching out to others—with sincerity and love—can make a difference in someone's day. Yours, too.

For Journaling:

There is convincing psychological research to demonstrate that kind and helpful behavior toward others brings meaning to our lives. The more we reach out to others, the more we achieve a sense of purpose and commitment in our own lives. When done on a regular basis, reaching out to others helps us meet basic psychological needs such as feeling close to others and a feeling that we are good and capable. Take some time and congratulate yourself on a kind deed done for another human being. What feelings do you have? How has your attitude changed or improved?

Think About . . .

The rowan tree in England has many associations with magic. One of its Celtic names is *fid na ndruad*, which means "wizard's tree." Believe it or not, you, too, are a wizard. When you wake up in the morning you automatically have the power to create some magic in another person's day.

Acknowledging Your Burls

You don't expect trees to change,
you love them as they are.
—ISABEL ALLENDE

On a research venture to gather information for a book on the longevity of multiple species of old trees (*In Search of the Old Ones: An Odyssey among Ancient Trees*), I journeyed to the Black River of North Carolina. On a calm and slightly overcast day, my guide and I took a kayak into placid waters in search of bald cypresses—trees that have existed for more than two thousand years in this peaceful ecosystem. Clustered along this iconic river is a vast acreage of soaring timbers that have stood against time and winds long before the arrival of humans. They are majestic in their years and beautiful in their stature. Theirs is a world tranquil and composed.

Eventually, the kayak bumped up against one of the towering bald cypresses. Sweeping my eyes upward, I noted several burls along its ascending height. Burls are common among these trees, each a prodigious growth in which the wood grain has produced a distorted protrusion or rounded outgrowth. Often the result of injury, fungal infection, or some form of stress, they are often viewed as deformities, botanical imperfections.

In truth, they are accents on the longevity of these trees.

Bald cypresses live for long years. The oldest, a giant deep in the solitude of the Black River, has lived continuously for 2,631 years (as of 2025). Its long life is due to its resistance to rot, the infusion of protective tannins throughout all its cells, and a solidarity against frequent storms and hurricanes that often topple lesser species. Its characteristic burls add character and dimension to this oldster. They are not deformities but rather botanical accents on a life well lived.

As you might imagine, constant attention on our imperfections is a focus on negativity. And frequent negativity drains us of our emotional energy; it consumes valuable time that would be better used elsewhere. Rather than being grateful for what we have, we complain about what we don't have. Yet the real joy of life is a knowledge that we can always improve, we can always grow . . . like trees.

I'm quite comfortable with my burls (age spots, hair loss, artificial knee). They don't disfigure me; they just make me unique. You, too, probably have a few burls that make you a singular individual—just like an ancient bald cypress along the Black River in North Carolina.

Accept your imperfections and you embrace a life of possibilities . . . a life of continual growth.

In Practice:

Journey into a nearby forest or wooded glen. Observe closely the differences between trees of the same species. What differences do you note? What are some flaws or defects between various trees?

- Are there imperfections in the bark—holes, scrapings, missing pieces?
- How is the structure of branches different? Do they all go in the same direction? Are there any missing branches? Are some broken?
- What about the splay of roots? Are some shorter than others? Have others been eroded or splintered?
- What about the arrangement of leaves on different trees? Are some discolored or others missing?
- What about the height of various trees? Are some taller than others? Have others been shortened by storms?

Undoubtedly, you'll notice several burls, several differences. Trees, too, have imperfections. That doesn't make them any less spectacular or magnificent. The same holds true for humans.

For Journaling:

What makes you unique? What distinguishes you from everybody else? In what ways do you stand out in a crowd? Take some time every now and again and write about one or two of your own burls in a positive way. For example, you may wear eyeglasses in order to correct your vision ("Ever since I was fourteen, I've been wearing glasses"). Perhaps you don't like this factor of your life. However, know that you are in a clear majority since more than 63 percent of adults in the United States wear prescription eyeglasses. You're part of a special group of folks. Celebrate that fact; make it a positive affirmation ("Those glasses have helped me enjoy and appreciate the art my wife creates").

Think About . . .

Box elders are often held in low regard. Brittle limbs, twisted trunks susceptible to rot, and dull yellow leaves often put this species in the "ugly tree" category. Perhaps box elders exist to remind us that if we continually think we're not as good as everyone else, then guess what? We'll continue to act as though we're not as good as everyone else.

Appreciation from the Inside

Why are there trees I never walk under but large and melodious thoughts descend upon me?

—WALT WHITMAN

A few years ago, I was contracted to write a children's counting book featuring majestic redwood trees (*Tall Tall Tree*). It was to focus on various creatures (salamanders, woodrats, banana slugs, etc.) that lived in the canopy of these botanical skyscrapers. But, at the beginning of the writing process, I was stuck—I couldn't seem to generate any creative ideas. So I decided to do something different. I imagined that, instead of observing these iconic trees as an outsider, I would mentally crawl inside a towering redwood tree and look at the surrounding environment as if I were in the center of that tree.

While "inside" the tree, I asked myself several intriguing questions. *What creatures would be crawling over my surface? How would the wind feel against my bark? What birds would be roosting in my branches? What kinds of insects would be creeping up my trunk?*

In short order, the ideas began to flow like warm maple syrup on a stack of Saturday morning pancakes. I couldn't write fast enough. After about three dozen drafts over the next eight to nine months, I eventually sent the manuscript off to my editor and the book was published to many positive reviews. My "inside/out" strategy had given me a unique perspective on some iconic animals and their distinctive environment.

That same strategy can also give us a similarly unique perspective on our own lives.

If someone asked you about the most important thing you have ever done in your life, how would you respond? Most people, when asked, would single out an external event. They would identify a competition or situation that was recognized by others via an award, a certificate, a medal, or a trophy. But how many people would identify self-improvement as the most important accomplishment in their lives? How many people would state one of the following?

- I have learned to be more patient with other people.
- I have learned how to live with my imperfections.
- I have been able to reduce the amount of stress in my life.
- I now take time for myself each day.
- I have discovered an inner peace I never had before.
- I share more compliments with my family.
- I think more positively about myself.

When you think about it, we often identify personal accomplishments in terms of how others perceive them. Our friends and family can see the new business we started. They can see the certificates that hang on the wall. They can see the new house we purchased in a nice neighborhood. The bigger question becomes "Are our greatest accomplishments those that can be *seen* by others or those *appreciated* by ourselves?"

Each day, give yourself at least one positive affirmation. Here are some possibilities:

- "I do good things for other people."
- "I love myself as much as I love others."
- "I am an important person in the lives of others."
- "I am proud of who I am and who I am becoming."
- "I make time for myself."

Write each on a Post-it note and place it on the top of your computer monitor, vanity, or kitchen cupboard before you go to bed. Make it the first thing you see the following morning.

You may discover that this simple activity reaps tremendous rewards. It gives you the opportunity to celebrate the most significant aspect of your life—your growth and development as a human being. It is also a signal that one accomplishment can trigger other equally important accomplishments.

All too often we waste considerable time seeking the praise and approval of others. More meaningful and more satisfying is the recognition of the internal progress we are making. Know that hanging a certificate on your office wall is less important than patting yourself on the back for quitting a bad habit such as smoking or eating too much sugary food. It's external recognition versus self-praise.

Looking at yourself from the inside out can be a positive affirmation of who you are and what you believe.

In Practice:

Schedule a time every so often for self-reflection. Find a calm place and quiet time to mentally review some of your internal goals and accomplishments. This procedure takes about five minutes, but it makes a big difference. Celebrate yourself, re-affirm the good things you do, and recognize your role in the lives of others. Here are some statements to get you started:

- Today, I will do my best.
- I deserve to be loved by others.
- I accept myself for who I am.
- I am capable of making good choices.
- I have dreams I want to pursue.
- I am a good person.
- I can forgive myself for my mistakes.
- I have boundaries and they are important.
- I am a strong person.
- I am allowed to experience pleasure in my life.

This self-review gives you direction and guidance on what is truly important.

For Journaling:

Write one personal accomplishment you've done this past week (parallel parked the car on the first try, helped a neighbor rake the leaves, sent an e-mail to a long-lost friend, helped a little old lady obtain a box of cereal from the top shelf in the grocery store, taught your son how to throw a baseball). How did you make yourself a better person? What did you do that you've never done before? Now, give yourself a pat on the back, a standing ovation, or a celebratory hug (don't forget the selfie). You deserve it.

Think About . . .

Constantly seeking the approval of others is a recipe for emotional disaster. A sugar maple tree doesn't need anyone's endorsement to produce maple syrup. It has the potential to be sweet just as it is.

Your Choice

Today I have grown taller
from walking with the trees.
—KARIE WILSON BAKER

I was born in 1947, thus making me an official senior citizen. What I find interesting is that according to the U.S. Social Security Administration, American men born in 1947 had an average life expectancy of 64.57 years. Thus, I have apparently exceeded expectations . . . but not as much as a grove of bristlecone pine trees in the White Mountains of California.

For several thousand years, bristlecone pines have prospered in this remote mountain enclave while humans have fought wars, established civilizations, and claimed territories across distant continents and ancient lands. These botanical stalwarts are famously regarded as the oldest trees in the world. Most exceed three thousand years of age and nineteen of the trees are more than four thousand years old. However, there is one oldster that has been scientifically measured to have germinated around 3050 BCE; thus, its age is well over five thousand years old.

And it is still living.

Not only is the age of bristlecone pines remarkable, so is the environment in which they live. Their territory is one that would be entirely hostile to most forms of plant life. These arboreal stalwarts thrive at an altitude of over ten thousand feet, the region gets scant rainfall, icy winds blow in during long winter months, heavy snows lay thick upon the land, freezing temperatures are the norm for many long months, the soil is primarily infertile, and the trees are constantly exposed to extreme solar radiation. Suffice it to say, these trees have withstood environmental conditions that would try the patience of any home gardener.

They thrive in spite of their conditions.

In an odd way, I was reminded of bristlecone pines when I picked up some clothes at the local dry cleaners the other day. It was obvious the clerk was not enjoying her day and was, most likely, not enjoying her job. A greeting from me elicited a frown and a grunt. She did not smile nor wish to engage in any type of conversation. It was quickly apparent that she was having a really lousy day. And she let me know it.

I, instead, choose otherwise.

I'm a strong believer in one of Eleanor Roosevelt's most famous quotes: "No one can make you feel inferior without your consent." That is to say, if someone chooses to have a bad day, that's not necessarily my day. Just because someone is grumpy, sad, moody, disrespectful, or irritating doesn't mean that I have to be that way, too. Most times, I choose to have a most positive day: pleasant conversations with my wife, a long walk through a deep forest, a loving phone call with my daughter or son, a creative writing project, a delightful dinner at a new restaurant, or just some me time to meditate or daydream. Someone else's day is not what I choose; I choose how my day will be lived and how my day will evolve.

Grumpy people are not part of that equation.

I suppose, by this point, you may be wondering about the connection between dry cleaning and bristlecone pine trees. Frankly, it's all about longevity.

According to recent research by psychiatrists at Yale University, concrete evidence shows that stress can have negative health consequences beyond the usual mental or physical health conditions. Their research demonstrated that, unequivocally, chronic stress can shorten one's lifespan. One of the researchers pointed out, "Some lifestyle choices mitigated the negative effects [of stress]. Subjects who showed strong emotional regulation and self-control skills had younger 'biological ages' than their counterparts who did not."

In short, a reduction of everyday stressors can have a positive impact on our overall longevity. Ancient bristlecone pines have effectively adapted to the stressors in their lives. As humans, we also have the capacity to extend our lives—specifically, by choosing the type of day we are going to have. Adding the stressors (e.g., bad attitudes, disagreements, moodiness, grouchiness) of others into our day does not contribute to our overall longevity. They choose their day; you have the right to choose yours. Nobody should do that for you.

Just something to consider—from a senior citizen.

In Practice:

Throughout our days we often meet folks in a bad mood. It's inevitable. Here are some recognized, and positive, responses:

- Share a compliment.
- Don't absorb their energy; stay calm.
- Counter their attitude with an accolade.
- Hold on to the responsibility for your own mood.
- Know that their bad mood is not your fault.
- Change the conversation.
- Walk away . . . smiling.

For Journaling:

Consider this quote: "For every minute you are angry you lose 60 seconds of happiness" (Ralph Waldo Emerson). In your journal, write your own version. For example:

- "For every minute I am ________________ I lose 60 seconds of ________________."
- Or consider a more positive rewrite: "For every minute I am ________________ I gain 60 seconds of ________________."

Hold on to these statements. Review them every so often.

Think About . . .

When walking through woods, you'll notice that each of the trees has its own unique shape, dimensions, roots, branches, and leaves. No two trees are identical, which reminds me that we each approach the world a little differently. We each have a choice.

Beauty Reveals Itself . . . in Time

I don't want to be a tree.
I want to be its meaning.
—ORHAN PAMUK

It had been a brutal winter. Icy blasts came down from Canada and froze both ground and creatures. Curtains of snow fell for days, obscuring vision in all directions. Day after day of punishing winds pummeled the land. It was an endless winter—dreary skies filled with gray and a landscape frozen in time and space.

The winter persisted. Endless weeks turned into endless months. It was a climactic and punishing assault from which there was little relief. Spring, such as it was, came slowly that year. It was in no hurry. Its voice was muted, its entrance subdued. Thermometers registered increasing temperatures—one patient degree by patient degree—a signal that change, a most reluctant change, was coming. The frozen grip would not give up easily, lasting well into April, extending the misery and anguish far too long.

Each day, on my way to teach undergraduate students, I drove past an eastern redbud tree. Divested of leaves, it had a constant cloak of icy crystals upon its branches. Piles of snow often built up around its base. It stood alone at the edge of a sweeping cornfield gilded in white—a solitary figure against a barren horizon.

Temperatures rose. Spring was on the way. Each day, I slowed to gaze . . . to watch for the grand unveiling.

Finally, that day arrived. I could sense its importance. As I approached, I could feel a spirit in the air. Then, there before me, in a brilliant explosion of color, was a glorious tree. Striking and robust pink flowers covered every branch—brightening the world around. The tree had changed; the cloak of spring embraced it completely.

The tree's brilliant pinks contrasted with the starkness of the land. This was a botanical ballerina—a debutant in all her radiance, all her finery. The tree had taken its time—but it was time worth waiting for. I preserved the memory with a dozen photographs.

Sometimes we, too, need time—time to emerge from a cocoon, time to grow and develop, and time to become . . . just become. Hurrying the process is counterproductive. Or as someone once said, "Good things come to those who wait." Our growth and development as human beings are never something to be rushed. Neither are those processes the same for everybody. We all learn to talk at different paces. We all learn our ABCs at different paces. We all learn how to interact positively with our fellow human beings at different paces.

Sometimes we just need a little more time to blossom. But, oh, what beauty awaits!

In Practice:

Personal growth does not have to be a solitary quest. Be sure to invite friends and family members to join you on your journey. When you do, you are building a support group founded on love and affection. Also, be sure to reach out to professionals or local support groups where you live. They can offer advice and counsel for your journey. Here are a few organizations available in almost every community:

- Grief share groups
- Addiction resource groups
- Recovery houses
- Mental health organizations
- Counseling services
- Behavioral help services
- Anxiety/depression treatment centers
- Marriage counseling
- Family counseling

For Journaling:

Far too often we see events in our lives as negative. *I'm seriously overweight. Why is it difficult for me to make friends?* or *I wish I could have all the money that Janet has. Then, I'd be happy.* Reframe those events or circumstances differently—look at them as incentives to take action or make changes. Instead of dwelling on your imperfections, view them as opportunities to improve. For example, you may wish to write this in your journal: "I'm seriously overweight." Underneath, formulate your statement in positive terms: "I will join the weight control group at the local hospital." Perhaps you might write, "Why is it difficult for me to make friends?" A possible follow-up statement might be, "I will seek some counseling at my local YWCA."

By reframing your *negative statements* into *positive actions*, you are creating a personal action plan—one that can reap many benefits. Instead of dwelling on your imperfections, use them to foster some new directions. Then give yourself some time to get to where you want to go.

Think About . . .

Ever notice how trees are always reaching for the sun? Charlie Chaplin put it this way: "You'll never find a rainbow if you're looking down."

Beginning the Day with Calm

And into the forest I go to lose
my mind and find my soul.
—JOHN MUIR

Every spring, tens of thousands of visitors attend the National Cherry Blossom Festival in Washington, DC. Folks wander along the Tidal Basin to observe and marvel at some of the most alluring trees in the world. Long expanses of Japanese cherry trees—approximately 3,750 of them—festooned with veils of pink and white cherry blossoms elicit a pantheon of *ohhhhhs* and *ahhhhhs*. Millions of photographs are taken, along with an equal number of selfies. It is a magical experience for all—a time to appreciate one of the great wonders of nature.

Many pause for a moment to contemplate and admire these magnificent trees. People take a few minutes to observe a single tree, a stretch of time to soak up the array of colors, or an extended intermission in silence and contemplation. Most visitors feel a decided loosening of tension, a stress-free admiration of natural beauty, or a necessary hesitation in their fast-paced lives. As you might expect, smiles are rampant, and peacefulness cloaks the land.

The contemplation of Japanese cherry trees each spring underscores my favorite time of day. Each morning I'm up at 6:00 AM and at my desk by 6:30 AM. Dawn is usually breaking, and the sunshine is sweeping over the landscape. Outside the large window in my office is a panorama of trees, a sweeping expanse of grassy knolls, and clusters of shrubs here and there. The world outside is quiet, as is the world around me. This is my time: time of reflection, time of contemplation, and time to slowly enter the forthcoming day. It is my solitude—long before my wife wakes, long before e-mails begin to pile up, and long before any obligations need to be satisfied. I have time—and opportunity—to reflect, to dream, or just to consider . . . nothing at all.

I am at peace.

Consider that a vital part of your daily routine might be at least ten minutes of downtime in every day. It may occur in the early morning, during your lunchtime, just after dinner, or while taking a stroll through the neighborhood. You may want to journey to a municipal park or other natural sites to walk with nature—to enjoy the beauty of a forest or the pleasure of a field of wildflowers. Whatever else is going on in your life, your quiet time gives you opportunity to practice inner peace and inner tranquility—every day. Your time alone helps achieve a sense of balance amid all the noise and demands of your day. By setting aside quiet time for yourself—every day—your batteries are recharged, and your spirit is lifted.

It is a mental break of incredible magnitude, a necessary intermission in the demands of everyday life.

A friend recently sent me a poem she wrote several decades ago. Its message is an essential part of how she begins her day. It underscores her philosophy of life and how she maintains her mental and emotional equilibrium. It is an ode to serenity.

Hands Off

The day dawned
  a moment ago.
Its offering of
  minutes and hours
    was laid at my feet.
Precious time . . .
  my own.
I raised a sign;
  it read, "Hands Off."*

A daily pause refreshes our minds, helps us sort out what is important, and allows us clearer perspective. Nothing will eliminate the tasks and responsibilities we must address, but a short break helps us cleanse our minds and slow down the action. Most importantly, it gives us a psychological and emotional anchor point. You will also discover that these breaks significantly reduce your end-of-day fatigue.

A daily pause gives you something valuable. In so doing, you can now give something valuable to others.

* © Beverly Read. Used with permission from the author.

In Practice:

Taking a break—pausing our desire to get everything done on our to-do list—has many positive benefits, particularly when we make it a regular activity (read: every day). Here are a few suggestions for your consideration: take a long bath, stroll through the park, read a spicy novel, say no, take a nap, plan a "nothing" day, make a not-to-do list, single-task (instead of multitask), prioritize a simple pleasure, meditate, or create your own quiet space. Each of these activities can decrease your stress, lower your anxiety, and reduce your depression. It's a daily habit with incredible mental benefits.

For Journaling:

From a psychological perspective, the pursuit of a leisure activity—especially one that is not productive, one that is done "just for me"—gives you control over your life. You make the decision, you are in charge of your activities, and you are in command of your feelings. Take time to record a favorite leisure activity (reading, walking, listening to music, daydreaming). In your journal, write down some of the personal benefits of that activity ("I'm more relaxed," "I'm more in touch with my true feelings," or "Life seems to slow down a little"). See if you can come up with three positives. Do this every week or so, and you will discover that regular pauses in your crowded life result in increased levels of self-confidence, renewed energy, and a more positive mood.

Think About . . .

A dwarf river birch never thinks it should be a flowering crabapple tree. A desert bloodworm tree never thinks it should be a blossoming cherry tree. According to an ancient Chinese proverb, "Tension is who you think you should be. Relaxation is who you are."

There Are No Magic Feathers

The trees will tell their secrets
to those that tune in.
—STEVEN MAGEE

The movie *Dumbo* (1941) is the animated story of a young elephant with very large ears who wants to fly but is afraid to do so. His friend, a mouse named Timothy, gives him a feather and tells him that the feather is magic, one needed in order to fly. Dumbo grasps the feather in his trunk and discovers that he can, indeed, fly. One day, while perched near the top of a circus tent, Dumbo accidentally loses the feather. The only way down is by flying, but he is terrified. Timothy urges him on, and eventually Dumbo takes flight. What he discovers is that the feather wasn't magic. Rather, the magic was inside him.

While the overall theme of the movie may seem simplistic when compared with the special effects and complex interactions of children's films today, *Dumbo* underscores a basic psychological concept. Consider our constant consumption of books, magazine articles, podcasts, and blogs in search of the secret formula that will make us eternally happy. Many self-improvement titles crowd bestseller lists—a sign that we are constantly searching for the magic elixir, the happiness formula, the door to a better life.

I am not suggesting that we give up that search. I am suggesting, however, that most guidelines and admonitions are based on a simple truth—*the potential for our lives lies within us.* Purchasing a book will not make us happy. Listening to a pop psychologist extol the virtues of a simple life will not guarantee joy. Watching a TED Talk on a new psychological movement will not ensure eternal satisfaction.

Fact: There are no magic feathers!

The ultimate factor for change in our lives lies within our hearts and minds. One of the most powerful things we can learn is to be grateful for who we are and to recognize the power within us. That growth process does not come about because of any external force or advice. It comes from within.

Consider the totality of trees. According to estimates there are approximately 3.04 billion trees in the world (that's roughly 422 trees for every person on earth). Botanists have determined that there are roughly 73,300 different tree species around the globe. Although there is a wide range of species in an equally wide range of locations, all those billions of trees share something in common: their growth comes from within.

A tree's growth is done via cell divisions in the cambium layer of the bark. The cambium comprises growth tissue cells just under the bark. Xylem and phloem cells are formed on both sides of the cambium and continually add a new layer each year. These visible layers are known as annual rings. Cells to the inside make up the xylem, which conducts water and nutrients. The fibers in xylem cells also give a tree strength in the form of wood. Cells to the outside of the cambium make up the phloem, which transports sugars, amino acids, vitamins, hormones, and stored food throughout the tree. In short, a tree's growth begins (and continues) from the inside to the outside.

So does yours.

In Practice:

Make a practice to schedule a day of celebration every now and again. Take the day off, get a babysitter for the kids, and go out and do something rewarding for yourself. Buy yourself a lunch at that new ethnic restaurant in town, get your hair and nails done at a fancy salon, take a long hike through a nearby forest, spend long hours at the park or a local coffee shop, get yourself some new earrings (okay, get that new dress, too), or take in a movie at a local theater. Do something for yourself . . . something that celebrates *you*! Most important: make those celebrations a regular practice.

For Journaling:

When you wake up in the morning, take a few minutes to recognize and celebrate yourself. Before your morning cup of coffee write something on an index card or record something using the Notes app on your cell phone . . . something you like or admire about yourself (for example, "I love and am loved," "I do good things for other people," "I love my sense of humor," or "I am learning a new skill"). Toss the card in a box. Do the same thing tomorrow . . . and tomorrow . . . and tomorrow. When you occasionally have a bad day, access your notes, stand in front of a mirror, and read them out loud. You may discover (or remind yourself) of some of your inner strengths.

Or you may want to sit down and make a list of your accomplishments in life. Your list should include everything—large and small (from the almost-perfect score you got on a second-grade spelling test, when you learned how to drive, when you set a personal record in running a 10K race, all the way up to the lemon meringue pie you made from scratch). What you will undoubtedly discover is that you have accomplished much . . . much to celebrate and much to cheer.

Think About . . .

South Tibetan cypress trees, native to the Yarlung Tsangpo Grand Canyon in southern Tibet, often achieve heights in excess of three hundred feet. Anthropomorphism aside, perhaps this is a reminder that our perception of how a day will turn out often becomes the reality of that day. In other words, if we want to grow tall, we can think it.

Not Giving Up

I'm like a tree. My leaves might change color,
but my roots are the same.
—ROSE NAMAJUNAS

Located in the village of Mouriscas in Centro, Portugal, is an amazing tree—an olive tree that is 3,350 years old . . . still living and still producing olives every year. As the oldest tree in the country, it has been classified as a Monumental Tree of Portugal by the Institute of Conservation of Nature and Forests. Year after year, century after century, it has fiercely clung to the earth. Each of those years it has produced a crop of olives.

It is tenacious. It is determined.

Growing up in Southern California, I was an avid sailor. One of my prized possessions was a Snowbird—a fourteen-foot class of sailboat I would frequently sail throughout the placid waters of Newport Beach. Snowbirds were originally constructed in 1921 and were competitive in the 1932 Summer Olympics in Los Angeles.

They were distinguished by a heavy wooden centerboard and a transom-mounted rudder. Near the top of the sail on my edition was a red letter "S" (for Snowbird) with the number "2" underneath (indicating that it was the second Snowbird sailboat manufactured—in other words, a "classic").

Each summer a sailing race—known as the Flight of the Snowbirds (since renamed the Flight of Newport)—is held; the regatta was first organized in 1936. One year, when I was about twelve or thirteen, and despite having a heavy wooden edition of the boat (all the newer boats were made of lightweight fiberglass), I decided to enter the race along with about a hundred other young sailors. Shortly after the race began, it was clear I would not be one of the top contenders. Ever so slowly I began to fall farther and farther behind all the other sleeker and lighter editions of Snowbirds. In the end, I finished more than a half hour after the winner. Dead last.

I slowly sailed home, tied the boat to the dock, gathered all my gear together, and slowly walked up to the house. I was crushed and dejected. My father, working in the side yard, met me, and I told him how the race evolved, how my boat got slower and slower, and that I had finished in last place. I was, quite obviously, not a happy camper. Then, with a slight grin on his face, he reached out and shook my hand. "Congratulations," he said.

It was a lesson I never forgot.

In Practice:

One of the best ways to become more determined or resolute is to set small, easily achievable goals for yourself. Too often, we give up (losing weight, for example) because we propose goals that are far too large or unmanageable. ("This year, I will lose sixty pounds.") Instead, make your goals more focused, more narrow. Here are some examples:

- "I want to write a book. I will start by writing seventy-five words a day."
- "I want to lose some weight. I will start by eliminating one hundred calories a day from my diet."
- "I want to run in a marathon. I will start by running a half mile every day."
- "I want to be a great Italian cook. I'll start by learning how to cook pasta al dente."

Keeping your goals small and manageable ensures greater success and more positivity in your life.

For Journaling:

Every so often, take some time and record one or two things you do well. For example, "I make the best pot roast in the neighborhood," "I take my arthritis medication every day," "After months of practice, I can now run a 10K race in less than fifty minutes," or "I completely understand my daughter's math lesson and can help with her homework." These may be little things, but if you add to your list over time, you will discover that you have embraced the concepts of determination and willpower in many different aspects of your life. Celebrate that!

Think About . . .

Dig a deep hole. Plant a tree. Fertilize it regularly. Water it frequently. Guard it from hungry animals. Remember that perfection is seldom achieved, but improvement is always possible. Something to think about every morning.

Two Old Friends Beside the River

Trees are as close to immortality
as the rest of us ever come.
—KAREN JOY FOWLER

It is a given that we do not live alone on this planet. We are social creatures, and we interact with one another on a regular basis. By the same token, we also take care of one another, either physically or emotionally. That's just the way we are.

Truth is, we each have a responsibility to our fellow humans. Our lives are not ones of solitude; they are ones of cooperation and collaboration. Since we live together, the implication is that we must also support one another. A community thrives when we look out for one another.

So the question becomes "How can I be of service to others?"

Helping others is a genuine act of kindness and generosity. It is a philosophy of living that assists others without the need for recognition or adulation. It is a process of reaching out and supporting those who may need a hand or those whose lives may be ones of struggle and survival. Helping others gives us purpose and direction, making the world a little better.

One day while walking beside the Roaring Fork River on the Western Slope of Colorado, my eyes were drawn to a ragged line of old-growth firs bordering the river's edge. In short order, my eyes caught two trees in close proximity. One was standing straight, holding fast to the earth with strength and determination. The other was canted to the side—tilting against its neighbor at a forty-five-degree angle. Its lean, I guessed, was the result of a violent wind or a calamitous storm that loosened its grip upon the earth. Several roots were exposed, indicating that it would have toppled to the ground were it not for the arboreal support of its neighbor. Fortuitously, the top branches of the two friends were locked in a decided clinch—one friend supporting the other in its time of need.

I could only guess how long the two trees had embraced each other—one depending on the strength of the other for its continued existence. I projected that they would remain in their positions for some time, one friend giving of itself so that its neighbor might thrive in a challenging environment. Together, they would ride out future storms, rising waters, and wild winds . . . intertwined . . . year by year.

Helping others can come in many different forms. It may include formal service activities such as working for a volunteer organization in your local community, donating money to a charitable group, giving your time to a service group, donating clothes or household objects to a local charity, or offering labor or goods to a housing project for homeless people.

Informal opportunities might include picking up litter along the road, speaking to a county service group, reading a book to youngsters at the local library, staffing a call-in center, helping an elderly person across the street, or simply giving a smile to someone who hasn't experienced a smile in a long time.

The most important aspect of community service is that it should be a regular occurrence. Giving back is not a singular event—it is a commitment to doing things for others on a consistent basis. It is a selfless act of understanding, compassion, and assistance that has no time limitations or restrictions.

What you will discover is that your life becomes fuller and richer. So, too, will the lives of others. It is a reciprocal relationship with benefits on both sides. What you give is also what you will receive. Service to others will produce greater levels of peace and joy in your life as well as in the lives of those you help. It's a mutual support system.

Just like those two old friends in Colorado.

In Practice:

One of the best gifts we can give anybody is the gift of time. Not money, not prizes, not material goods—just a slice of time. Making time for time offers opportunities to positively affect the lives of others. Donating a piece of your day to others enriches their lives as much as it will enrich yours. Time could mean a lifetime of service or an hour or two at a community agency, bringing a little sunshine into someone's day. Think about some ways in which you could donate a little piece of your time to make the lives of others a little better . . . a little richer. Contact your local county office and ask for a list of volunteer agencies and organizations. A local church, synagogue, mosque, or temple will undoubtedly have some useful information for you, too.

For Journaling:

Here's a saying from Winston Churchill: "We make a living by what we get; we make a life by what we give." What do those words mean for you? In what ways are you able to give to others in your family, your community, or your work environment? Record your thoughts.

Or take the word *community* and separate out the last five letters. What does that new word tell you about the importance of giving back? Write your response. Share it with others.

Think About . . .

Observe a grove of aspen trees or a deep forest of evergreens. Notice how the trees stand together in close proximity to one another. Perhaps they are reminding us of the following two words—two words for a strong friendship or love affair: *always there.*

Count All Your Riches

We can learn a lot from the forests,
regrowth, change, and beauty.
—CATHERINE PULSIFER

A few days ago, I received an e-mail announcing that if I clicked on the link in the message, I could assure myself of "a magnificent life filled with great riches and much happiness." Soon after, another e-mail popped into my inbox informing me that I "could make thousands of dollars (and earn great recognition) every month with very little work and very little time." I couldn't send both messages to the spam folder fast enough!

Millions of these scams proliferate across cyberspace every day. As you know, they are designed to obtain personal data and effectively siphon money out of bank accounts. For those of us who use the Internet in our work, there often seems to be an unending stream of these scams.

These messages are all based on a basic human desire for a forever joy. Too often, we look to monetary rewards as the ultimate determinant of happiness. One consumer investment group recently reported that fully 18 percent of the American public are basing their retirement plans on hopes they will win the lottery. The astronomical odds of a grand prize apparently hasn't deterred many individuals banking on a massive jackpot for their retirement nest egg.

Easy winnings, easy life!

Ironically, the more time we spend chasing after free money, the less time we spend being happy. When we reorient our goals to the natural pleasures of life—the little things that all too often we take for granted—our happiness quotient escalates. Indeed, some of our greatest assets are often right in front of us. Absolutely free.

Not too long ago, my wife, Phyllis, gifted me with a long weekend stay at a beautiful B&B on the Eastern Shore of Maryland. Fronted by the Chesapeake Bay and graced with vibrant stands of red cedars, American beeches, maples, oaks, and tulip poplars, it was a visual wonderland that calmed the soul and refreshed the mind. On one of our travel days, Phyllis and I discovered the Eastern Neck Wildlife Refuge about a dozen miles south of our lodging. We crossed an overwater bridge, parked the car in a tiny parking area, and set out on a sinuous trail through a thick and handsome forest. The calming was instantaneous, and the quietude allowed us to hear the gentle flap of wings and an occasional scurry through the underbrush.

As we walked through a diversity of trees, we made many discoveries, including several examples of Texas live oaks. These evergreens are impressive with their sprawling branches, leathery lanceolate leaves, and egg-shaped acorns. Rapid growers, with a large canopy of shade, they are also known for their adaptability to many soil types. They also live for several centuries. But it was their towering majesty that captured us. Their silhouettes against a crystal blue horizon commanded the cameras on our iPhones, and the reach of their leafy branches held us in constant awe. We were swept up in their grandeur and delighted to discover something new in a previously unknown ecosystem.

We were rich with emotions.

Discovering new elements of the world we live in is a reminder that some of our greatest rewards might be right in front of us. It is often a great revelation to discover that the simple things in our lives are also our greatest riches. The first time our child says *mama* or *dada*, a greeting card sent by a long-lost friend, a brilliant sunrise, a surprise dinner from a spouse, a hug from a grandchild, a compliment from a total stranger, a walk in the woods—these are the true riches of life.

Too often, we take simple things for granted when they may be our greatest rewards.

In Practice:

Realize that your daily happiness might be right in front of you. It will seldom arrive as an e-mail from someone you've never met, or a "business" bent on extracting your personal information for its own nefarious ends. More than likely, happiness can be found in your living room, the kitchen, the backyard, just around the corner, or just down the road at a place you've never been. Strive to begin each day with an appreciation of one element, one person, or one event already in your life. Consider the following:

- A playful dog
- A baby's laugh

- Flowers in your garden
- Your next-door neighbor
- A tall tree in the neighborhood
- A walk in the park
- A family member
- A good meal
- Your life

Honor what is close at hand, and you will feel refreshed and revitalized.

For Journaling:

Think about some of the important things you might take for granted: your spouse, your significant other, your kids, the house, your job, your neighborhood, and more. Take a few moments, and write about one of them in your journal. Then compose a short essay about how your life might change if that was no longer there, no longer available. For example, what if your job was completely eliminated, how would your life be different? What if a family member died suddenly? Record your response.

What you might discover is that when you take something for granted, you often don't give it the importance or appreciation it deserves. Consider how that might change your attention to that item. What could you do to demonstrate more gratefulness for each of the items on your list? For example, how could you show more gratitude for your spouse or significant other? Record your response.

Think About . . .

The two squirrels were frantic! They chased each other up and down the nearby fir tree and across its extended branches. Occasionally they stopped, looked around, and then continued their antics for many long minutes. It's interesting to note that some of life's great pleasures sometimes arrive without advance notice.

What Do You Like About Yourself?

Forests may be gorgeous
but there is nothing more alive than a tree that
learns how to grow in a cemetery.
—ANDREA GIBSON

Phyllis and I occasionally visit the small parish of Humshaugh in northeastern England where our daughter and her family live. A tiny town with fewer than a thousand inhabitants, Humshaugh was founded in the thirteenth century under its original name of Hounshale ("Hūn's nook of land"). It is close to Hadrian's Wall, and The Crown pub in town is a popular spot for hikers visiting this ancient Roman artifact.

In the center of Humshaugh is St. Peter's Church; originally built in 1818, it is a stone-faced structure sporting a well-weathered exterior, occasional patches of moss, and the overwhelming stillness of age. Surrounding it is a congregation of several species of trees that have been on-site since the church's initial construction. We sometimes take time to stroll through these trees, observe the well-worn grave markers, and marvel at the architecture of this splendid edifice. At various junctures, I've found myself pausing beside several old English oaks admiring their stature and magnificence. What have they experienced in their more than two centuries of living? What events occurred beneath their branches?

I suppose that these regal organisms—throughout their years—most likely stood up to many challenges, including fierce winds, robust rainstorms, and other natural assaults. It would seem likely that, in spite of those hazards, they also have much to celebrate. They grew tall, they grew long branches that reached out in myriad directions, they added immeasurable beauty to the church grounds, they held the earth firmly in place so that graves could be preserved for long periods of time, they burst forth with a profusion of leaves and new growth each spring, and they were admired by town residents as well as visitors from afar. Their longevity, I suspect, is due to an internal resiliency—an evolutionary buffer against events that would diminish them, or perhaps even topple them.

We all go through times when things do not go our way. The clerk at the department store may not treat us as kindly as we would like. The person who returns our dry cleaning may not be in a good mood. Someone may cut us off in traffic. A supervisor may not return a message or provide a service we asked for. We often take these events personally. We sometimes take offense, and our mood changes accordingly.

Too often, we carry around bad feelings about a negative event or encounter. We may even internalize those events and say to ourselves, *Gee, that person doesn't like me,* or *I must have done something wrong. Maybe it was my fault.* The actions of others may shape how we think about ourselves. Often those beliefs tend to wear us down because we carry them around for extended periods of time.

A friend, Sharon, maintains a personal diary. In it she writes her thoughts, ruminations, and feelings about her life and the teaching career she has chosen. On Monday mornings, though, she does something different. She gets up fifteen minutes earlier and uses that time to write something special in her diary. She always begins it the same way: "Three Things I Like About Myself."

Sharon has discovered that this small bit of time reflecting on the things she enjoys most about herself is her buffer against the world around her. She says that by taking the time to accent her strengths and reinforce the goodness within herself, she can face the week with renewed energy and a reinvigorated self-concept.

Know that by taking time to celebrate the things you *know* to be true about yourself, you obtain approval from the most important person in your life—you! What you think about yourself and how you celebrate that knowledge can be powerful motivating forces for the days or weeks ahead. With a strong internal resiliency, you can stand strong against the challenges ahead.

Some trees in the north of England have much to celebrate, too.

In Practice:

Frequently remind yourself that your frame of mind is best determined by you, not the actions (or inactions) of others. Don't allow others to drive your life; make the journey one of self-determination. Here's a related quote I particularly enjoy: "I learned a long time ago the wisest thing I can do is to be on my own side" (Maya Angelou).

Worrying about the opinions of others is nonproductive and self-defeating. It does not move your life forward; rather, it slows you down and allows self-defeating thoughts to take over. So when someone treats you unfairly, ungraciously, or rudely, stop for a moment and record one of your positive attributes or signature behaviors. Do it immediately after the event. It will make a difference.

For Journaling:

To deflect negative thoughts, take a few moments at the start of each week to record one to three things you like about yourself. You may wish to record these on the Notes app on your iPhone, an Excel spreadsheet, individual index cards you keep in the top drawer of your desk, or in your journal. Every once in a while, take a peek at those statements. Use that brief moment to remind yourself of the things that make you special—the strengths you recognize in yourself.

Think About . . .

Hawthorn trees will always be short—seldom reaching more than twenty feet in height. Yet their early summer blooms are amazingly beautiful. How often do you celebrate the life you have, instead of bemoaning the things you do not have?

No Sweat

Be like a tree and let the
dead leaves drop.
—RUMI

There's a saying that's been around for a long time: "Don't sweat the small stuff." Although this maxim has been part of the American lexicon for several decades, we still don't practice it; we still don't understand all its implications. In our multitasked life, we quite often sweat the small stuff simply because the small stuff crowds our lives and becomes bigger than it really is.

Remember the guy who tried to cut in front of you at the bank? Or how about the lady who bumped her cart into yours at the grocery store? Or consider the server at the new restaurant in town who forgot to bring you a refill on your drink. Or maybe you recall when you sent a birthday card to a grandchild and never got a thank-you note in return. Or that time when someone made an inappropriate comment about you on Facebook. All small stuff. All relatively inconsequential. All minor events. Yet we often make them a big deal and blow them way out of proportion. We *do* sweat the small stuff, and in so doing, we turn tiny issues into major problems.

We increase our stress; we decrease our happiness.

It's not life that is a bummer; it's our attitude toward life's little incidents that consumes our time and wastes our energy. Rather than letting those events go and getting on with our day, we allow them to consume our thoughts. Nothing constructive is accomplished; our emotional energies are diverted to events that mean little in the grand order of things.

In the southwest corner of Tasmania lives a slow-growing species of trees known as Huon pines. They have been around for more than 100 million years—from a time when the Australian continent was much farther south and much warmer than it is today. Now, Huon pines are found primarily in riparian environments, in areas with high rainfall, and on ground periodically subject to flooding. They attain heights of up to ninety-eight feet with long and arching branches, and spirally arranged leaves.

But their ultimate claim to fame is that they are often cited as some of the world's oldest living trees. In 1955 a stand of these trees, on Mount Read in western Tasmania, was determined to be in excess of 10,500 years old. Each of the trees in the stand is a genetically identical male that has reproduced vegetatively; each is a clone of every other tree. While the stand has existed for more than a hundred centuries, researchers at the Royal Tasmanian Botanical Gardens report that individual specimens within that stand live for "just" three thousand years.

During its existence, the Mount Read Huon pine grove has undoubtedly endured several events—most minor, most inconsequential to its extended life. Occasionally, a branch, heavily weighted, might crack. No sweat—a tree continues its growth! It's certain a bird, or flock of birds, have left their droppings on selected sections of individual trees. No sweat—those trees survive year after patient year. Typically, the forest experiences a dry period. No sweat—the rains eventually return with necessary hydration. As animals pass through the forest, they may scrape off some bark. No sweat—these trees are infused with the chemical compound methyl eugenol, which helps preserve the timber and prevent any rotting.

All minor events, nothing to get excited about! Huon pines continue their lives . . . through centuries and beyond millennia.

No sweat!

In Practice:

When we spend too much time on the small stuff, we lose sight of the big picture. Our attention is diverted, and our goals are compromised. Knowing that there will be tiny interruptions in our lives gives us reason and the rationale to deal with them quickly. In other words, reorient your life to the major events; don't sweat the small stuff. Here are some strategies for your consideration:

- Think about how a particular event might matter a week from now, a month from now, or a year from now. Most likely, it will have little, if any, influence over your life. Let it go.
- Often, when we get caught up in the minor events in our lives, we lose focus on the larger, more important issues. We spend too much time wrestling with small stressors and end up ignoring the values and beliefs that keep us grounded. Spend some time writing what you truly believe. Review (and add to) that list every so often.
- When you find yourself perseverating on one or more little things, grab a pen and write down two or three objects of your

gratitude (e.g., your health, the love of your children, a friend who confides in you, a smile you shared with a stranger). You'll notice a shift in focus, a reorientation back to the important things in life.

- Write the following Swedish proverb on a slip of paper. Tape it to the corner of your desk or the side of the bathroom mirror. Read it often: "Worry gives a small thing a big shadow."

For Journaling:

You more than likely have many stressors in your life. Lots of events or circumstances crowd your day and wear you down. Here's a suggestion: Take a little time and record all of the stressful events in one day of your life. Afterward, you'll undoubtedly discover that most of them were quite minor. You forgot your keys when leaving the house, you miscounted your laps while swimming at the community pool, a friend forgot to share some technical information you requested, you put on a mismatched pair of socks, you bought the wrong brand of peanut butter at the grocery store, you stepped in a puddle while crossing the street, or you forgot to pick up some milk on the way home from work. Minor events. In fact, most of the items on your list are, most likely, very small. Nothing to sweat about.

Stuff happens. Quickly erase. Proceed forward.

Think About . . .

It's certain that the suicide tree (*Cerbera odollam*), used in private landscaping projects in India, should probably have an alternative name. What a disappointment! Do you have a disappointment in life . . . a minor disappointment? Write it on a slip of paper. Set it on fire. Now it's gone, time to move on. Oh, be sure to clean up your ashes!

On Patience

The trees that are slow to grow
bear the best fruit.
—MOLIÈRE

The morning was ashen and drizzled. The thick fog hanging outside the kitchen window blotted the sun and obscured vision in every quarter. The viscous gray was ever-present; drabness prevailed.

I stood in the kitchen—a carafe of Kona coffee brewing on the counter. I stared out the window and saw . . . nothing! A ponderous mantle of mist wrapped each house with a gloomy pallor. The weeping cherry tree that dominated our front yard was swallowed by the fog—lost in a murky atmosphere reminiscent of old horror movies with baying wolves and a naïve couple stranded on a puddled country road at midnight.

We had tenderly planted our charge several years earlier. The anticipation of pink flowers highlighted each spring. But now, the fog all around obscured its presence. It would not reveal itself. I was frustrated.

Often we are in a hurry to get through our day—to get through life. We fill our agendas with so many meetings, appointments, engagements, and lists of other scheduled activities, that we scarcely have time to enjoy life. For many of us, each day is a mad rush to put check marks on our to-do list. We become so consumed with getting as much accomplished as we can in twenty-four hours that we seldom have time to notice the world where we live. We are stressed. We are anxious. We are constantly rushed and often impatient.

To become a more peaceful person, slow down and embrace patience as a daily objective. Take some time to observe, feel, experience, watch, ponder, wonder, and contemplate. The way to happiness is to insert more serenity into your day—to slow down your schedule and ease your tension. In turn, your blood pressure will decrease and your spirit will escalate. You'll notice a greater satisfaction with who you are and where you're going. Patience is the key to a happier life and an inner peace.

I stood in the kitchen, coffee cup in hand, and waited. After about fifteen minutes, the mist sluggishly began to dissipate, and the tree gradually emerged into the day. It was full of bright pink blossoms. I smiled, walked upstairs to my office, and contemplated other possibilities.

In Practice:

Being more patient, particularly in our multi-tasked world, is a constant challenge. Here are some recommendations from psychologists to help you incorporate more patience into your day:

- Be aware of what you can control, and what you can't.
- Put fun or play or both into every day.
- Practice mindfulness.
- Insert more optimism into your day.
- Walk as a way of slowing down and contemplating.
- Spend more time listening, less time talking.
- Be willing to accept your mistakes.
- Don't take life too seriously.
- Meditate.
- Respond, instead of reacting.
- Reconsider deadlines.
- Practice gratitude every day.

For Journaling:

Regular journaling offers you a unique opportunity to slow down your thoughts and ponder everyday events more deeply. So, too, is journaling useful in helping you track your progress over an extended period of time. Throughout this book, each essay has a journaling activity that, when practiced faithfully, can help you include more patience in your life.

For this activity, select one of the items from the In Practice list above and record your answers to the following two questions: In what areas of your life (home, work, neighborhood, travel, etc.) would you be able to insert your selected item? How would that item be beneficial to you over time?

Think About . . .

Always remember that one of life's greatest pleasures is raking up a big pile of leaves and jumping in with your kids. Trust me, the trees won't mind one bit.

Our Interpretation of Failure

Anyone who thinks fallen leaves are dead
has never watched them dancing on a windy day.
—SHIRA TAMIR

Some of us embrace challenges and disappointments as opportunities to refocus our thinking. These are folks with a *growth* mindset. Then some others see any failure as—well—a complete failure. They believe that they never had the talent or skill anyway, and they probably never will. These are folks with a *fixed* mindset. These individuals embrace the belief that people are either born with certain talents or not.

Convincing research shows that most of us intentionally place ourselves in one of those two groups. And the group to which we have assigned ourselves frequently determines how we respond to many of life's challenges. If we experience failure and give up, then we have conveniently assigned ourselves to the fixed group; if we experience failure and use that as a learning opportunity or stepping-stone to improve, we have placed ourselves in the growth group.

I fondly remember an excursion along a trail in Appalachia. While walking past a riverbank crowded with magnificent American Elms, I discovered a tree that had succumbed to the ravages of age, weather, climate, and violent thunderstorms. It was lying prone on the damp earth, cloaked in a thin blanket of moss along sections of its trunk. Clumps of ferns poked up haphazardly from the surrounding soil. Two frogs peeked out from inside a cavity near its base. The remnants of a bird's nest lay in its crown. A solitary slug tugged its way over a naked root on a mission to seek sustenance or a potential mate. And all around was an array of tiny sprouts—an indication of new life and new beginnings.

I observed this once mighty titan and the neighborhood it inhabited. I was taken by the fact that its death (or its "failure of life") now offered creatures and sundry plants a new opportunity for living. The horizontal tree, deprived of life, was giving life back to others in its orbit. In human terms it embraced a growth mindset—using its final failure as an opportunity for growth by others.

As you well know, failures are an inevitable condition of our daily lives. We missed the left turn on our way to a friend's house; we forgot to pay the electric bill on time and are assessed a penalty; we make a New Year's resolution to lose twenty pounds and six months later we are still at the same weight. It's how we approach that failure that determines whether we are fixed in our thinking or ready for some growth. As you might imagine, people who believe they are members of the growth group tend to be more successful than those who self-assign themselves to the fixed group.

Consider Thomas Alva Edison. In the latter part of the nineteenth century, Edison was attempting to improve the light bulb. For more than two years, he experimented with a host of potential filaments to discover an element that would sustain light. Sometime during this arduous process, a newspaper reporter interviewed him. He asked Edison, "It seems as though you've tried and tried to invent the incandescent light bulb and continue to fail each time. Why is that?" Edison looked the reporter square in the eye and said, "I have not failed. I've just discovered 10,000 ways that won't work."

Knowing that we will encounter failures in our lives is a healthy perspective. But how we deal with those failures can provide us with the inner peace and emotional satisfaction we relish. With practice, we can learn that most failures are simply learning opportunities. Instead of crying out, "I'm a complete failure," we can do an about-face and look at a misfortune as a chance to improve—an occasion to alter our course of direction. Instead of moaning over the forgotten electric bill, we could use that experience as an incentive to develop a spreadsheet recording when bills are received and when they need to be paid.

When you take time to rethink your mistakes as learning opportunities, you give yourself a special present: the realization that one of the most distinguishing features separating success from failure is that successful people make mistakes and use them as learning opportunities while unsuccessful people make a mistake and stop. Most people consider success and failure as opposites; in reality, they are both part of the same process.

An American elm falls on the ground: failure.

A fallen American elm offers sustenance and shelter to others: success.

In Practice:

When faced with a personal or professional challenge, we often generate restraining statements that give us permission to give up (*I can't do this, That's way out of my league,* or *Apparently, I don't know very much about that*). Instead, ask yourself questions that generate multiple possibilities. (*What if there was more than one way to figure this out? What if I looked at this from another point of view?* or *If it was possible, how could I . . . ?*) This reorientation puts you in that all-important growth mindset.

For Journaling:

Everyone in the world has flaws, imperfections, and peculiarities. So, too, all of us make mistakes, boo-boos, and bad decisions. Know that those traits make us all human. Accept that and you're on the road to a life of peace. Use that fact as a launchpad for improvement and discovery, and you're on the road to personal success.

For practice, pen a recent mistake or failure that you experienced. For example, you purchased the wrong shade of blue at the paint store. Write how you might view that event in a positive light (Maybe *I got the wrong paint color, but perhaps the Jamisons might want to use it for their new baby's room*). Maybe you put in new plants along the driveway, but they all died. Your response might be, *I think they were in the wrong kind of soil. I'll check with the lady at the garden store to see what kind of fertilizer I should have used.* By writing down your failures and then reframing them in positive terms, you may discover that many of your mistakes can lead to new discoveries. You'll also discover that many of your mistakes can lead to learning opportunities. From time to time, you may wish to review your journal entries and note your progress.

Think About . . .

The baobab trees of Madagascar, Africa, and Australia are also known as upside-down trees due to their unique appearance. A good reminder that I'm okay and you're okay. Neither one of us is perfect—and that's okay.

Compassion Is the Greatest Gift

Love is like a tree, it grows of its own accord,
it puts down deep roots into our whole being.
—VICTOR HUGO

Several years ago, I received a note from a friend that a former college student of mine (whom I call here Daria) had been diagnosed with stage 3 stomach cancer. Daria had been an outstanding undergraduate who wrote compelling and insightful papers and actively participated in every class with enormous perception. She was loved by all, and I was certain she would make a significant difference in the educational lives of children. She would be a model teacher and a model individual, and indeed the teaching profession welcomed her with open arms. She was truly an exceptional educator.

After reading the note, I sat down and wrote her an e-mail. I reminisced about her positive contributions to our college classes and her devotion to the highest ideals of the teaching profession. I expressed sympathy for her recent diagnosis, knowing that it would affect both her personal life as well as her professional responsibilities. I took time to let her know how much she was loved—not only by former classmates and current students, but by an old professor, too.

In about a week, I received a reply. In it, Daria said that the timing of my message was perfect. She was in a program of chemotherapy with radiation therapy to follow. She was extremely tired and mentally exhausted. Her prognosis was not optimistic, and she was constantly struggling with the effects of her disease. She told me that my message was full of love and hope and that she planned to hold on to it and read it several times in the weeks and months ahead.

A few months later, Daria returned to her classroom and her students—still full of the spunk and positive attitude that made her such an outstanding classroom teacher. Subsequently, she and I agreed to meet every other month or so to talk teaching over tall cups of latte at a local Starbucks. In those meetings she and I shared some of our teaching challenges, such as educational conundrums that impacted our creativity, along with other professional issues and personal concerns. She was seldom without a smile, compliment, or insight, and I always left those coffee sessions full of hope and possibilities. She was always inspiring.

The word *compassion* is defined as "a sympathetic consciousness of others' distress together with a desire to alleviate it." You will quickly note that this definition is composed of two elements: a *recognition* and an *action*. It is a realization that the lives of others may have heartbreak, pain, or frustration. Their problems may be as real as ours, but sometimes they may be worse. This recognition helps us realize the need to open our hearts and offer our hand. It helps us realize our connectedness.

I am reminded of something I read many years ago. It went something like, "Remember that everyone you meet has their own set of problems, issues, worries, and concerns. Your compassion might lift their load a little. By the same token, so, too, will your load be lighter as well."

Consider olive trees—some of the world's oldest living trees (3,500-plus years). They exist in arid and hostile climates, are often bent and crooked, and grow in areas with poor soil. Yet they give. Their fruit has been cultivated for more than 8,000 years, their oil is one of the most common cooking ingredients in recipes around the world, and olive trees have served as an inspiration for celebrated painters such as Vincent van Gogh, who created fifteen paintings of them.

Olive trees give back throughout their long lives. Their needs are few, yet they offer so much—and they've been doing that since before the birth of Aristotle and the founding of Rome. Perhaps one of the lessons of olive trees is that compassion is a necessary attribute—one we can all learn and practice. It doesn't have to be complicated or complex. A smile at a stranger on the street, a kind word to a clerk in a store, a shared laugh with a delivery person, a donation of time to a local volunteer group, a note to a former classmate, or maybe a shared cup of coffee every now and then.

Less than three years after we began our coffee conversations, Daria passed away at the age of thirty-two. Soon thereafter, I received a message from her mother inviting me to deliver a eulogy at Daria's memorial service. I began my remarks with the following: "Every once in a while, someone walks into your life . . . and changes it . . . *forever.*"

In Practice:

Are you in crisis? Are you dealing with an issue that consumes your time and your thoughts? Try this: Write yourself a note and let "you" know that you are there for "you." Offer yourself some support and encouragement. Give yourself a "pat on the back." Share a positive thought or a note of encouragement. Put the note in an envelope and mail it to yourself. Do it again next month. Watch what happens.

For Journaling:

Stop! Right now, sit down and write a letter or note (not an e-mail or text message) to someone in crisis. It may be someone you know dealing with a disease, a divorce, a family issue, or a financial struggle. Let them know that they have your support and understanding. Tell them that you are in their corner. Mail your note to them right away. Don't wait, don't tarry. They need to hear from you, now.

Think About . . .

Botanists tell us that one mature tree, on average, produces about 260 pounds of oxygen every year. Contemplate that fact in light of this quote from Ralph Waldo Emerson: "to know even one life has breathed easier because you have lived. This is to have succeeded."

In Awe

In all things of nature
there is something of the marvelous.
—ARISTOTLE

The dictionary defines *awe* as "an emotion of veneration and wonder." The Greater Good Science Center at the University of California, Berkeley, defines awe as "that goose-bumpy sensation that we get in the presence of something profound: something greater, more powerful, or more eternal than ourselves. It arises when we encounter things that challenge our sense of what's normal or possible." According to several researchers, awe is often associated with participation in or observation of extraordinary events: seeing Arches National Park for the first time, being in the presence of a famed musician, or experiencing the sacred during meditation. But its true influence is in everyday events such as the change of colors in autumn leaves, sighting the Big Dipper when camping, the birth of a lamb, the first robin of spring, or a father pushing his handicapped son's wheelchair across the finish line of a local marathon.

A vast cluster of scientific studies have proven that experiencing awe stimulates wonder and curiosity. So, too, is awe influential in reducing the impact of inflammatory chemicals on the immune system. But most critical are psychological discoveries that convincingly demonstrate that awe improves our well-being and contributes to more positive attitudes for ourselves, neighbors, associates, and family.

The human mind aside, the heart experiences awe as something beyond words, beyond belief, and often beyond conscious learning. It is as much an emotion as a fact. It is something experienced rather than something described. It is both an amazement as well as an enlightenment; it delights as much as it elevates. Above all, we are changed—for the better!

On my first sighting of Japanese maples, I was in deep admiration. Every step through their wonderland revealed beauty and splendor in ways that sucked the air from my lungs and widened my eyes into large saucers of wonder. The journey, weaving past gorgeous trees, was similar to hearing a classical performance—a soaring crescendo of botanical notes that ignited the senses and piqued the emotions. These trees embodied the grace of nature and the epitome of its splendor.

Japanese maples are a must-see experience. They are glorious, majestic, and impressive—a species that inflames the senses and delights the soul. The ability of these trees to arouse awe is one of their signature features; the experience is beyond mere emotion or casual observation. Walk through these trees, and you will be transformed, forever changed.

Contemplate the implications of awe in your daily life. Does it occur rarely, or is it something you actively seek or embrace?

Does it lurk within the silliness of a shoeless dance you do with your grandchildren? Do you find it slinking through the rich soil of your vegetable garden? Or perhaps, if you slow down just a little, you can see it in the ripples across a tranquil forest lake. An attention to awe allows you to focus on the simple things of life, the mundane events we take for granted all too often: a field of wildflowers, a swarm of butterflies, a soaring mountain, the laugh of a youngster at play, the nuzzle of a friendly puppy, or just holding your spouse's hand while shopping. All are awesome!

In turn, you may discover something else: being in awe is being alive.

In Practice:

Yes, Japanese maples are awesome. But so, too, are the trees in your backyard or neighborhood. Stand beneath those trees, and contemplate what might be awesome about them. Do their leaves strike your fancy? How is one tree's bark significantly different from another's? What do you see in the splay of roots? Use your cell phone to take photos or record your thoughts.

If you'd like to inject more awe into your life, consider the following books: *Awe: The New Science of Everyday Wonder and How It Can Transform Your Life* by Dacher Keltner (2024) and *The Power of Awe: Overcome Burnout & Anxiety, Ease Chronic Pain, Find Clarity & Purpose—in Less Than 1 Minute per Day* by Jake Eagle and Michael Amster (2023).

For Journaling:

If you were a tree, what would others find awesome about you? Do you stand tall and straight? Do you create a song when the wind blows? Are you a sanctuary or place of safety for others? Do you lead a colorful life? You may want to pen some of those awesome features and save them in your journal. Feel free to add to your list over time.

Think About . . .

The next time you stroll through a vast evergreen forest or gaze at a flowering tree in the spring, remember that the best gifts in life seldom come in a wrapped box with a bow on the top.

Part II

Leaf No Stone Unturned

Life Isn't Fair!

There is always music amongst the trees . . . ,
but our hearts must be very
quiet to hear it.
—MINNIE AUMONIER

How many times have you said to yourself the old refrain "Life isn't fair"? I caught myself the other day when two publishers had rejected a book proposal I had worked on for several months, my car developed some sort of mysterious engine issue, and I received word that a dear friend had just lost her job. All in the same day. Yeah, life truly isn't fair. Sometimes it just stinks.

One of the biggest mistakes we make is comparing ourselves to others, seeing others as having more luck than we do. For example, we judge our efforts against a friend who writes a bestselling novel, a neighbor who receives a major promotion at work, or a fellow runner who wins a major competition. This behavior is, as you might imagine, self-destructive. In those instances, we often confuse "fairness" with "entitlement." We fall into the trap of believing that some people get *all* the breaks while others are doomed to a life of failures and doubt.

When we get into that life-isn't-fair funk we begin to feel sorry for ourselves, we build up a mountain of self-pity, and we groan about all the injustices in the world. Our mood shifts dramatically and begins to affect our work and our social relationships. We wallow and complain, sinking deeper into self-induced behavior that benefits nobody—especially ourselves.

The bottom-line reality is that life has never been fair and will continue not being fair far into the future. How we recognize and accept that reality ultimately determines our personal satisfaction. Realizing that things aren't always going to turn out the way we think they should is a healthy attitude. Understanding that there will always be bumps in the road or barriers to hurdle is a positive way of embracing our lives now and going forward.

Setbacks and disappointments are inevitable, and our attitude toward them is controllable.

Rocky Mountain National Park is an expanse of superlatives. Rich and engaging vistas combine with a diversity of wildlife to make this national park one of the most visited in the country. On high mountains visitors encounter the distinctive limber pine, a tree that inhabits elevations of seven thousand to eleven thousand feet. This environment is harsh, brutal, and unforgiving. The trees often endure long winters of extreme cold, powerful winds, and minimal access to water. The trees frequently cling to rocky outcrops in some of the most windswept areas of the park. The unyielding wind often gnarls and twists tree trunks into unique shapes and distinctive symmetries.

For the limber pine, life isn't fair.

But it has been able to adapt—quite well—to this brutal environment. One of its most distinctive features is its flexible branches, which allow the tree to cope with powerful and relentless winds emblematic of high elevations. These trees also have extremely long taproots that anchor them around the edges of towering cliffs or along the perimeter of alpine lakes. Their height—only fifteen to thirty feet—is an additional barrier against powerful gusts and constant squalls. For the limber pine, life certainly isn't fair, but it copes by making necessary ecological adjustments and modifications.

We need to accept the fact that life isn't fair. In turn, we can use that acceptance as a stimulant to improve not only what we have but the world around us. That's simply because the unfairness of life is something everyone deals with—you and me and about 8 billion people in the world. By reaching out and helping folks in a similar reality, we can contribute something positive to the lives of others as well as to our own. Doing so is also an act of empathy for them and a personal reward for ourselves: a win-win enterprise.

So instead of pondering the myriad injustices life has for us personally, we should remember that we are all in the same boat. Life isn't fair for everyone, but we can make it better, for others and ourselves, one considerate action at a time.

In Practice:

Whether life is fair or not is a choice. It's something over which we have a certain level of control. For example, you can choose to treat others fairly, you can choose to not spoil the environment, you can choose not to cheat or defame others, and you can choose to give accolades and respect. You can embrace the concept of fairness in how you deal with others. You can help with the unfairness in others' lives by offering recognition, support, and celebration. Their lives and yours will become fairer.

For Journaling:

Accept the fact that life isn't fair—for anybody! But know that what you do with that realization will make the biggest difference in your life and the lives of other people in your orbit—friends, family members, colleagues, even strangers on the street (remember, their lives aren't fair either!). The fairness in your life is all about how you improve the fairness of life for others. In your journal, record some of the things you can do for others that will improve their lives, put them in a better mood, alleviate one of their burdens, or hold their hand in a time of stress. Or answer this question: *What can I do to bring more joy, happiness, or satisfaction into the lives of those I live or interact with?* Bottom line: The fairness of your life will improve in direct proportion to how much you improve the fairness factor in the lives of others.

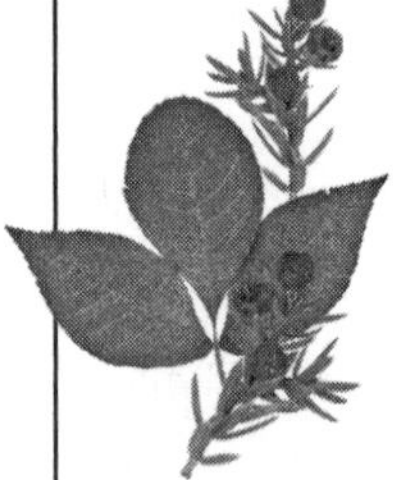

Think About . . .

A southern magnolia tree planted in New Hampshire may grow, but it won't bloom. Here's another reality check: Life is rarely the way we want it to be. Get over it! Move on!

Facing Your Regrets

You are a child of the universe,
no less than the trees.
—MAX EHRMANN

On one of our day trips to a local park, Phyllis and I held hands and strolled a trail through a resplendent forest of trees. Arching branches festooned with bright green leaves, the scamper of small animals among the detritus on the ground, and the swirl of a summer breeze through this hauntingly beautiful enclave gave us pause to stop and admire the wonders of nature far from the madness of crowded highways and the blare of civilization.

The muddy path wound among magnificent stands of white oaks, silver maples, and flowering dogwoods. It was a world apart, a world of peace and serenity. But as we turned a corner we saw a stunted tree—one considerably shorter than its contemporaries. It had fewer branches and even fewer leaves. It was clearly struggling to survive in an environment that welcomed more decorative members. Were it human, it may well have regretted its location, its stature, or even its life. "Woe is me!"

In 1969 Frank Sinatra recorded a song titled "My Way." In it are the following lyrics:

Regrets, I've had a few
But then again, too few to mention

What about you? Do you have any regrets in your life? A lot? Or too few to mention?

One of the most powerful emotions all humans share is that of regret. The regrets of our lives carry with them a lot of emotional baggage and negative thoughts. There are two primary types of regrets: regrets of *commission* (having an affair, driving while under the influence, losing our temper with a five-year-old, saying something inappropriate to our best friend) and regrets of *omission* (not completing college, not taking that vacation to Tahiti, not fixing the car when you should have, not thanking your parents for their sacrifices). Quite often we carry those regrets around for a very long time. They weigh us down and can depress our moods for decades.

But as frightening as regrets are, they can also be an incentive to alter our behavior, embrace optimism, and better our lives. First, as with unfairness, everyone has regrets. They're universal. You and your friends and neighbors—and total strangers—are all regretful. The ability to recognize that fact of life is critical to your mental health.

Second, consider that tiny tree in the forest. It may be smaller than its contemporaries, it may have fewer branches and fewer leaves, but it has survived—quite well. It is anchored in the soil, it can withstand strong winds and brutal storms, it can take in vital nutrients and water, and it can stand its ground. It perseveres in spite of the environmental challenges it faces.

In Practice:

When considering the regrets of your life, know that they are perfectly normal. In fact, several psychologists suggest that considering our regrets can be a healthy way to view our lives. For example, a regret can give you specific information about a part of your life. That focus can then be an incentive to motivate, inspire, and guide you toward a personal change, a life improvement. Acknowledging your regrets helps you focus on possible strategies that might allow you to deal with your omissions and commissions.

Your value is not the sum total of your mistakes but rather your willingness to accept your feelings—and use them for change. Before you start your day, consider the following quote: "to give back to ourselves—there lies the great, singular power of self-respect" (Joan Didion).

For Journaling:

Write a letter to yourself forgiving you for something you've done, something you now regret. This task is difficult but an important one. It does, however, give you opportunity to let go of the disappointment, anger, or resentment you may have toward yourself. Rather than continually beating yourself up, you are practicing self-compassion—using the same level of kindness, forgiveness, and understanding you would use with a friend or family member. Keep your letter in a safe place and refer to it every so often as a reminder that you are in control of your feelings. They don't have to control you.

Think About . . .

Oak trees can regenerate lost limbs. Oaks often sprout new branches from buds close to a wound when they are pruned or when a branch breaks off. You can regenerate, too. Consider these words of advice: "You can't turn back the clock. But you can wind it up again" (Bonnie Pruden).

Other People's Problems

Earth and sky, woods and fields . . . teach some of us more than we can ever learn from books.

—JOHN LUBBOCK

As I was driving to the dentist's office one morning on a foggy rural road slick from an overnight ice storm, I needed to cautiously navigate the hills and blind curves. I was going along at a safe speed for the conditions when a pair of headlights rapidly approached behind me. In a few moments the driver was directly behind me with not more than a few inches separating our bumpers. It was obvious the driver was in a hurry and thought that if he tailgated me, he would be able to increase my speed and get to his destination faster.

The road provided no opportunities for the car to pass nor for me to pull over. I became increasingly nervous about his dangerous driving. I worried that an animal might run in front of my car—or I might slide on an icy curve—and the tailgater would plow into my car.

As I became more anxious about the situation, it occurred to me that I was allowing his inconsiderate behavior to become my concern. His inability to maintain a safe speed on a slick road was now becoming my problem. I began to realize that other people have the potential to increase our stress in many ways. Their attempt to control us by exerting pressure on us enables them to alleviate their own immediate problem. In short, we become their victims at our own expense.

Type "terrible trees" into any search engine and near the top of the list will be the Bradford pear. This is a tree that horticulturists hate, gardeners despise, and arborists abhor. Its reputation, such as it is, stems from the fact that it is a species that chokes out native trees throughout the East Coast. Bradfords also crowd out vegetation that native wildlife depends on for food. Its flowers smell like fish, and the trees explode in windstorms. Bradfords cause economic and environmental harm wherever they grow—and they propagate faster than a warren of overactive rabbits. According to one expert, "If you have a Bradford pear in your yard, yesterday would have been a great day to cut it down."

Bradford pear trees give new meaning to the term "invasive species." They control roadsides, run rampant over the landscape, and prevent any other trees from gaining a foothold. They are pushy, domineering, overbearing, and dictatorial. If they had a motto, it would most likely be "My way or the highway!"

Some people are like Bradford pears. They run rampant over our emotions, they invade our minds, and they exert their power over our lives. They impose their will, often to our detriment, and they are domineering, often to our frustration. They should be avoided at all costs.

However, we should not become inconsiderate individuals as part of that process. Rather, we should avoid assuming the responsibilities of others who would expect us to compensate for a deficit in their actions, character, or attitude. We understand that ultimately we are responsible for ourselves, not for the actions (or lack of actions) of others.

Just because the driver behind me on the road has a problem, I do not need to provide his solution. My immediate concern is to maintain a safe driving speed and arrive at the dentist's office safely. The individual behind me needs to take responsibility for his poor planning. It is not my problem but his.

In Practice:

Someone else's bad day does not have to become your bad day. Take some time—preferably as soon as you wake up—and decide what kind of day you're going to have. Make a conscious decision and commitment to the tenor of this coming day. If you start off with the sincere belief that today will be a good day, it sets a positive tone for all your commitments and obligations. You choose your day. Don't let others choose it for you. Make it your day—your way!

For Journaling:

One of the responses we often have toward disrespectful people is to blame them for our unhappiness. We complain and criticize others for our unhappiness and sour mood. We try to push the pain away by faulting others. Your response should not be one of hatred or distrust of others but rather in treating yourself as a loving and giving individual. It's all about practicing self-love—listening to your inner voice and taking action on behalf of yourself. Instead of advocating for others to change (a frustrating process, to be sure), address your own needs and your own feelings. Use your journal to record some of the self-love actions you can do during the day. For example,

- I take a time-out every so often to thank myself for what I'm accomplishing.
- I frequently give myself a mental hug for how I'm able to communicate with others.
- I really like it when I can make other people smile or laugh.
- I try to maintain a positive attitude when I meet people for the first time.

In short, celebrate what you have, not what others want you to be. Ultimately, your happiness is not dependent on others. It's dependent on *you*!

Think About . . .

It was a tiny sprig tenaciously clinging to a cairn of rocks in the harsh and brutal environment of Acadia National Park in Maine—a reminder of the following: "We are shaped by our thoughts; we become what we think" (Buddha).

Searching for Happiness

The clearest way into the Universe
is through a forest wilderness.
—JOHN MUIR

Like you, I wouldn't mind having a larger investment portfolio, an estate overlooking a pristine beach in Hawai'i, a sumptuous yacht, a private jet, and an annual three-week vacation in Tuscany. All those things would be wonderful additions to my life; truth be told, though, they would be false additions to my happiness. They would be a way of saying that I can buy my happiness instead of creating it myself. It would be a focus on what I *want* instead of what I *have.* And once you have those things, you continue to want and want more—expanding your acquisitions but denying your ability to create your own happiness. This only expands your ongoing list of desires, which, concomitantly, expands your dissatisfaction with what you have.

We often believe that our accumulation of bling will ensure a life of happiness. The more things we obtain, the more happiness in our life. That belief often turns into a vicious cycle where we continually purchase more and more and wind up with less and less. It's a constant cycle of dissatisfaction covered over with more and more toys. When we continually want more things, we often ignore the treasures we already have: a loving spouse, a roof over our heads, sufficient food, a healthy lifestyle, the love of our children, and a means of employment.

Now, pick a forest, any forest—one close to where you live or one in a new territory. Take some time and walk between the trees. Observe closely and you may notice the calmness there. There is serenity between the trunks and a peacefulness that stands in stark contrast to our rushed lives. Most trees reach for the skies, gathering in the sunshine while a tangle of roots zigzag through the soil absorbing water.

This is a placid realm. The animals that inhabit this environment scamper across a carpet of leaves, squeak and squawk from tall trees, hide in holes deep in a titan's trunk, or skitter across the worn bark of an ancient giant. Life is gentle, vibrant, and continuous. Food is sufficient, nutrients are plentiful, and survival is ensured. Creatures of every magnitude find their home here. Their needs are met; they live in a sustainable world. They have what they need; they want for little.

Survival is ensured. Life is rich.

Perhaps there is a lesson in this forest wilderness. Perhaps the moral is that we should change the emphasis from what we *want* to what we *have*. In so doing, we might increase our happiness and alter our outlook on life in most magical ways. That change significantly decreases our chase for recognition based on our material assets to a celebration of what we have earned and what we should be grateful for. When we fall into the trap of *If I obtain more things in my life, my life will be happy*, we ignore what money can never buy: love, respect, honor, and, of course, true happiness.

A celebration of what we have shifts our focus from the impractical (or unlikely) to something over which we have more control: the here and now. Life's greatest satisfaction comes from an emphasis on our *haves* over our *wants*. When we spend our days wishing for things we don't have instead of celebrating the things we do, it's time to stop, rethink, and start over.

Celebrate all your presents in the present.

In Practice:

A state of personal happiness can be achieved when we work to bring happiness into other people's lives. A humorous comment, a cheerful disposition at work, a celebration of the achievements of friends and colleagues, a positive attitude about life, and a willingness to help others are actions we can all practice. When we actively help others have more happiness in their lives, something magical happens: We achieve more happiness in our lives. How about today? What is one thing you could do to make someone's life a little better?

For Journaling:

Create a list of those things that don't require purchases, but that bring you enormous satisfaction and contentment. These may include a newborn baby, close friends, a puppy, the smile of a stranger, the love of another person, a garden of flowers, Mexican food, holding hands, a phone call from the kids, a splendid sunset, the first snow of winter, mountain air, the laughter of children, or even a walk through the forest. Make this an ongoing list and add to it often—once a week or so.

Think About . . .

The Crooked Tree Forest grows in the village of Nowe Czarnowo in Poland. Remarkably, all the trees there grow in the shape of the letter J. You, too, don't have to follow all the "rules." Break a few from time to time. Make your own. Thomas Edison did. So did Marie Curie. And that physics guy—name of Einstein, I believe.

Giving Back

He that plants trees,
loves others besides himself.
—THOMAS FULLER

The redwood stood silent—a towering behemoth full of grandeur and presence. I paused for a moment, thoroughly drinking in its magnificence. I considered that for centuries this tree made its environment much better than when it first pierced the earth as a tiny sprout. Along with its compatriots, this redwood built strong arboreal communities, enriched the atmosphere with pleasant pheromones, absorbed atmospheric carbon, added immeasurable beauty to where it lived, and held the soil close so that other organisms—botanical and zoological—might benefit. This icon, in silent majesty, reminded me that we are all members of a sharing existence, regardless of whether we are lofty redwoods soaring to the clouds or wide-eyed humanoids strolling a northern California trail.

This tree constantly gives something to its ecosystem. I should do no less.

Phyllis and I lead a comfortable life. As a retired professor, I'm certainly not rich, but we have a roof over our heads, are able to put food on the table, drive serviceable cars, and can visit our grandchildren every now and again. Luxury Caribbean condos, expensive sports cars, and a personal butler are not on the agenda. We have what we need.

But we are equally aware that some people in our community are not as fortunate. Feeding their families is not as easy as going to the grocery store and purchasing whatever they want. They may live below the poverty line, be out of work, or struggle with an expensive medical issue or even a lack of adequate housing. They may live paycheck to paycheck, scrimping just to feed their children. Quite often, they may need to skip a meal, sending their children to bed without dinner.

For several years, we have given money to the local food bank. Each month a certain amount is deducted from our bank account and donated to a local agency that provides food to families in need. While we never have the opportunity to meet the families we may be helping, part of our reward is in knowing that their difficult lives may be enhanced just a little. That gives us a warm feeling and the satisfaction of knowing that others benefit enormously.

As members of a community, irrespective of age or station, we all have obligations and responsibilities to our fellow citizens. We do not live in isolation (unless we choose to do so) but rather as neighbors. As neighbors, we have many positive ways to help others with their necessities for daily living. It's an outreach to others less fortunate and a reaffirmation of what is truly valued in a community.

Of no less importance is the warmth you'll feel helping others. You'll feel better about others and better about yourself. Win-win!

In Practice:

Giving back to others has the power to inject some happiness in someone's day and, not surprisingly, more joy and satisfaction in your own day, too. A simple act of kindness can positively change attitudes as much as it changes outcomes. Before you start your day, consider the following quotes:

- "Kindness is the highest form of intelligence." —Unknown
- "Be kind, for everyone you meet is fighting a harder battle." —Plato
- "Tenderness and kindness are not signs of weakness and despair, but manifestations of strength and resolution." —Kahlil Gibran
- "No act of kindness, no matter how small, is ever wasted." —Aesop
- "Try to be a rainbow in someone's cloud." —Maya Angelou
- "How beautiful a day can be, when kindness touches it." —George Ellison
- "Kindness can transform someone's dark moment with a blaze of light." —Amy Leigh Mercree
- "We rise by lifting others." —Robert Ingersoll

For Journaling:

Consider celebrating those in your local community who are giving back to others. Write a letter to the editor of your city newspaper about the work of volunteers at a local agency. Contact a local radio station and invite them to discuss the value of volunteers. Send a thank-you card to the director of a rescue mission or food bank. Post a message on one of your social media accounts and let your followers know about a community group in your area. Make these missives a regular part of your journaling efforts, and you may just see something magical happen—for them and for you.

Think About . . .

Wildfires, insect infestations, and climate change are affecting large swaths of trees around the globe. In every country and municipality, trees are struggling to survive. Keep in mind that every person you see today also has challenges. See if you can address one of them.

Sharing Gratitude with Strangers

Finland is officially the world's happiest country. It is also 75 percent forest. I believe these facts are related.

—MATT HAIG

The other night, Phyllis and I, along with a dear friend, went out to dinner at one of our favorite restaurants. As usual, the food was fabulous and the service impeccable. When the check arrived, I added in the tip, totaled up the amount, and signed my name. I also took the opportunity to pen, "Thank you, Jennifer, for the great service," at the top of the bill.

I've long believed that people in the service industries do not get sufficient gratitude for the work they do. Postal clerks, cashiers, restaurant servers, nurses, plumbers, flight attendants, custodians, and so on, have to deal with grumpy, cranky, ill-tempered, crabby, sulky, irritable, complaining, snappy, grouchy, or just plain difficult people during the course of their workday. They regularly have to listen to tirades, outbursts, rants, diatribes, harangues, vitriol, swearing, and other less-than-pleasant comments from the public. It must wear thin after a while.

They deserve better.

Bringing a little sunshine into the lives of others is a pleasurable and rewarding experience. People who deal with complaints, special requests, and demands on their time are particularly deserving of a simple acknowledgment or friendly greeting. Spreading a little joy is a simple act, but it is more than attitude. It is more than a simple courtesy. It is also a belief—a belief that we can positively influence other people through simple words and simple actions.

But here's a greater realization: *Everybody* deserves some sort of gratitude. Every. Single. Day. A sincere "Thank you," a smile, eye-to-eye contact during a conversation, a note, a text message, a friendly wave, or just a simple, "How's your day going?" to neighbors . . . Expressing gratitude is, quite simply, a sincere recognition of the people in our lives—including family, friends, neighbors, and strangers. When we show appreciation, we demonstrate love. Equally important, we also develop an inner peace that reduces stress and enriches our soul.

On frequent walks through wooded environments, I'm constantly reminded of the giving nature of trees. Trees, and the forests they inhabit, provide shade, beauty, solitude, comfort, and peacefulness. Via photosynthesis, they create and release oxygen into the atmosphere so that humans can breathe. They offer ecosystems that sustain other forms of life, including mammals, fish, reptiles, amphibians, and birds. So, too, do trees enrich the soil, stabilize riverbanks, provide places of solace and contemplation, and harbor vast numbers of creatures in their canopies. In essence, they are essential to the survival of many forms of life, humans included.

The trees encountered on forest hikes can remind us of the value of gratitude as a daily activity, a daily practice. The important fact is that when the people around us are appreciated and feel genuinely valued for the things they do, they invest greater effort and energy into their jobs. So, too, do they feel better about themselves and their place in the world.

So when you are out and about, take a few moments to share some gratitude. Make someone's day a little brighter. Let them know that they are recognized. Celebrate their work. Value their role in the community. Applaud what they do. Share some appreciation. Smile. When you do, you'll discover something quite amazing:

Your day will be a little brighter, too. Guaranteed!

In Practice:

Want a good incentive to smile more at the people you meet? Smiling generates more positive feelings within you and significantly reduces your stress level. Several researchers have commented that smiling is, in many ways, similar to getting a good night's sleep or receiving a large sum of money.

Share a smile; enrich someone's life—and yours as well! Consider, if you will, this quote from celebrated comedian and pianist Victor Borge: "A smile is the shortest distance between two people." Just something to think about before you leave the house for work or run your errands for the day.

For Journaling:

The Broadway musical *Bye Bye Birdie* (1960) had a classic song: "Put on a Happy Face." The simple message was that when you put a smile on your face you automatically put a smile on your day. Interestingly, since that song was released, psychological research has proven that this suggestion contains a great deal of truth. Not only does a happy face give you incentive for your day, but it might improve someone else's day, too.

Journal about some of the smiles you shared with other people today. What exactly caused you to smile? How did another person react to your smile? How did the simple act of smiling make you feel during an encounter with another person? Perhaps you might want to rate some of the smiles you shared. On a scale of 1 to 10, how did you feel when sharing a smile with the local handyman, your spouse, the server at the coffee shop, one of your children, someone walking their dog, an individual at the local community center, or a stranger at the airport?

Think About . . .

Walk through an old-growth forest. Those trees have escaped the wrath of chainsaws and the invasion of bulldozers ever since they germinated. They are reminders that when we show respect and admiration for others, we give them the ability to grow tall. Like trees, when you cut people down, you destroy their potential for growth.

Living with Less

If we surrendered to earth's
intelligence we could rise up rooted,
like trees.
—RAINER MARIA RILKE

On a stony hillside just outside the city limits of Riverside, California, lives a most ancient tree—a solitary Palmer oak (*Quercus palmeri*), whose lifespan encompasses the invention of the wheel, the Trojan War, the Magna Carta, the bubonic plague, the Boston Tea Party, Lindbergh's flight across the Atlantic, and the onslaught of COVID-19. A research team from the University of California, Davis, compared the overall size of this tree against its annual growth rate and determined that this specimen had an estimated age of approximately 15,600 years.

Yet, as one of the longest-lived trees on the planet, it exists in a most challenging location. The surrounding environment is rocky, arid, and nutrient poor. Water is at a premium, and hot winds constantly blow in from the surrounding desert. Those winds by themselves are sufficiently powerful to stunt its growth—the tree is considerably shorter than any of its contemporaries. Yet, in spite of a significant lack of ecological resources relished by most home gardeners, this tree thrives—and endures—with less while we, as supposedly all-knowing humans, accrue more and more stuff.

Our lives seem to be ones of constant accumulation. We offer our children educational software and creative playthings—presumably sending them off to an intellectual life full of discovery. We buy ourselves the latest bling, the biggest houses, chic clothing, and expensive wines from European vineyards. We are a nation of rabid consumers bent on overspending and overt consumption. We seek to guild our lives with the biggest, the most admirable, and the most expensive.

Sometimes it seems as though we spend more time accumulating material goods and less time attending to our inner peace and happiness.

You may discover that if you take a little time every day to focus on what you can do to improve yourself—show more compassion, share some kindness with others, be grateful for what you have, exhibit respect for others, attend to your inner core, be more loving, share more hugs—you have more focus in your life. In doing so, you will have a clearer vision. You will enjoy your progression, step-by-step, celebrating the journey as well as the destination. Like the classic reggae song "I Can See Clearly Now" (1972), you'll have a daily purpose and a daily goal. You'll find it more satisfying to know that you're on a mental expedition full of possible discoveries and personal advancement. Remember, when you die, few will care what you have accumulated. They will, however, remember who you were as a person and the happiness you shared with others.

The Palmer's oak is evidence that constantly growing is considerably more productive than constantly accumulating.

In Practice:

We know that time spent in nature gives us opportunities to consider where we are and where we want to go. A walk in the woods or a stroll through a forest is a psychological stimulant of possibilities. Plan some time once a week when you can walk through a wooded glen, a deep forest, a grove of fruit trees, or even your neighbor's backyard. You'll discover that this time will change your mood, lower your heart rate, relax your spirit, and infuse your mind with all sorts of positive thoughts. So, too, will that time lower your stress, accelerate your creativity, offer more clarity, and improve your mood. Best of all, time among trees has been proven to significantly improve your happiness quotient.

For Journaling:

Here are two questions to answer in your journal: *How can I make my life a little better today?* and *How can I make someone else's life a little better today?* As daily objectives, the answers can offer you guidance and direction. They can move you forward *and* positively impact the lives (and days) of others. Consider recording your thoughts and reflections on a regular basis (say, once a week or so). As you begin to accumulate those entries, go back and read them. Try to determine what you have learned and what you can include as part of your everyday actions. You will, most likely, discover some amazing things to celebrate as well as others that just might need a little more work.

Think About . . .

Many olive trees live long lives—up to three thousand years or more. So, too, do these ancient trees continuously produce fruit throughout their existence. Their message is certain: enjoy what we have and produce much, instead of wishing for something unnecessary or irrelevant.

Make Compliments a Daily Habit

He plants trees to benefit another generation.
—CAECILIUS STATIUS

If you ask arborists for a specific tree species that complements a house, the silver maple is often cited. Its silvery leaves blowing in the wind are a visual spectacle. The silver undertones on its bark identify it as one of the most distinctively colored trees for any garden. In the fall, when its leaves turn brilliant shades of red and yellow, it becomes one of the most beautiful trees in the neighborhood. But perhaps its most outstanding complementary act is its leafy spread—arcing out for up to fifty feet in all directions. Its reach is perfect for family picnics and long afternoon naps. Urban, suburban, or rural, the silver maple is a wondrous addition to any home or municipal park.

If you want your life to stand for respect and kindness, it's always appropriate to share respect and kindness with others as a daily belief—as a daily habit. I like to do this by offering regular compliments to friends, family, colleagues, and associates. But I've also discovered many opportunities to compliment those I've never met: strangers I encounter when I run errands, do necessary shopping, am flying to visit relatives, or meet at the local drugstore. Complimenting others recognizes their worth and a celebration of their personal efficacy.

"You really light up the room with your smile."

Have you ever noticed how you feel when someone gives you a compliment? There's an inner glow, a feeling of being valued and respected, and an overall brightening of your day. Interestingly, psychological research shows that getting a sincere compliment gives us the same positive mental boost as receiving cash. More important, a compliment gives us feedback from others about how we are perceived, what other people think of us.

"Thanks for your patience. You really helped me with this application."

That same body of research shows that both the giver and the receiver of a compliment benefit, compared with how they felt beforehand. The person who received the compliment feels good as does the person who gives the compliment. It's a win for both parties.

"Your friends are lucky to have your positive spirit in their lives."

A few years back, a researcher sought to examine the likelihood of wedded couples divorcing or remaining together. Interestingly, when all the data were analyzed, the single most important determinant was the ratio of positive to negative comments that partners make to each other. The results showed that, on the one hand, couples who stay together have a ratio of approximately five positive comments for every negative one. On the other hand, couples who ended up divorced had shared significantly more negative comments than positive comments throughout the marriage.

"I absolutely love your sense of humor. You always make me smile."

Sharing compliments is one of the most positive ways we can connect with others. The key to a good compliment is to be specific; providing details can elevate a simple compliment into a memorable one. This holds true for people you know as well as those you meet in your daily activities or travels through the community. Compliments demonstrate recognition and respect. Best of all, they're easy to offer and should always be in good taste. Make someone's day—give them a compliment. It'll make your day, too!

"Thank you so much for bagging my groceries today. You really helped me out!"

In Practice:

When giving someone a compliment, don't focus on physical appearance. Instead, accentuate their core values as a person. Try complimenting someone on their kindness, curiosity, sense of humor, sincerity, helpfulness, listening ability, or confidence. Here are a few examples:

- "Talking with you makes my day."
- "You're so funny, you always make me laugh."
- "I admire your attention to detail."
- "You're a really kind person."
- "I love your sense of design."
- "You're a great listener. You always make me feel heard."

- "You're a terrific team player."
- "I'm so proud of you and what you have accomplished."
- "You're the happiest person I know. You're always smiling."
- "You're always upbeat. Your personality really shines."
- "You always challenge others to be better."
- "You always make me feel safe."
- "You make life so interesting—always an adventure."
- "You're an inspiration. You always go the extra mile."

For Journaling:

Giving compliments has emotional benefits for the receiver and the giver. The brains of both individuals release endorphins that positively affect mood, reduce stress levels, lower pain, boost self-esteem, increase morale, and decrease anxiety.

Before you start your day, try taking five minutes to record some possible compliments you could share with family ("I'm so proud to call you my daughter"), friends ("You are such a good listener whenever I share something personal"), coworkers ("I like the way you start your day with a positive attitude"), or even strangers ("Thank you so much for your attentive service"). As we've stated, be sure you frame those possibilities in terms of individual personality traits or characteristics.

Think About . . .

It was one of the most incredible trees ever—a splendid redwood standing along a puddled trail. It towered to the clouds, spreading its influence to all who stopped to observe. It was absolutely magnificent! Ever find yourself looking for the perfect gift? If so, give someone a compliment. They, too, will stand a little taller.

Self-Supervision

Love the trees until their leaves fall off,
then encourage them to try again next year.
—CHAD SUGG

As a professor of education, one of my duties was to supervise student-teachers. A student-teacher is a teaching candidate who has completed all their college coursework and is then assigned to a certified classroom teacher in order to "practice teach" for a semester. Once a week, I would travel to an assigned student-teacher's school and observe that person teaching a single lesson or a series of lessons. Afterward, the student-teacher and I would debrief—going over the lesson(s) and determining where it could be strengthened and where they, as future classroom teachers, could improve.

I usually opened each of the debriefing sessions with a most critical question: "If you were to score the lesson you just taught—on a scale from 1 (low) to 10 (high)—what number would you give yourself?" The query was often unexpected for the student-teacher, but I felt it was necessary. I'm a firm believer that frequent self-evaluation gives us opportunities to honestly appraise our own strengths and weaknesses. I wanted to give my student-teachers opportunities to reflect on their own work and, in consultation with me, identify necessary areas for strengthening.

After a student offered a score from 1 to 10 (for the time being, let's assume it was a 7), I would follow up with the question: "If you were to teach the lesson over again, what would you need to do to turn that 7 into an 8."

Initially a student-teacher would wrestle with that question, often because it's one seldom asked. And not only were they asked to rate themselves, but they were also subsequently asked to offer an improvement plan—actions or behaviors that would make the lesson more effective and students more successful. The student-teacher's response always gave us a most engaging opportunity to plan a viable course of personal and professional enhancements.

When I began my career I quickly discovered that the best teachers are those who have as much to learn as they do to teach. I often shared this maxim with prospective teachers, one I hoped they would embrace throughout their own careers. I also knew that the best kind of self-improvement always comes from within. We don't grow because someone tells us we must or because someone else seems to have all the answers to our challenges or problems. Self-help is a process that germinates and grows from inside. It's a belief in oneself, part of which is having the means and capacity for continuous growth.

I was thinking about the value of self-assessment in concert with self-improvement during a recent hike through a county park in the southeastern part of Pennsylvania. Along this bucolic trail, Phyllis and I came upon an enormous weeping willow tree that had secured its station along a meandering crystal stream. High, arching branches eventually bending over and hanging down are characteristic of this iconic tree. Majestic though it might be, it is frequently cited as a tree inappropriate for planting near homes. That's because, as part of its own constant "self-improvement program," the weeping willow extends itself in myriad directions. Long, sinuous roots reach ever outward, twisting and bending beneath the soil in their constant search for water—lots of water, which is why we often find them along the banks of streams and rivers. Homeowners eschew these trees because they ruin septic systems and damage sewer pipes, yet wanderers through forest enclaves celebrate their beauty and regalness with breathless wonder. Their subterranean search for water is constant, as is their unmistakable beauty and awe-inspiring stature.

As I did with my former student-teachers, you should also practice a regular program of honest self-assessment. Not surprisingly, you'll discover that this can be a most positive experience. Knowing where you are in the present can offer direction and incentive for where you can be in the future.

In Practice:

One of the most beneficial strategies we can employ on our quest for self-improvement is mindfulness. Mindfulness focuses on the here and now, where we are in the present and how we might be in the future. Regular time for mindfulness in our demanding world makes us more open to experiences that have been shown to aid our self-improvement. Suggested mindfulness activities include

- Mindful stretching: A series of stretching exercises that focuses attention on both breath and mind.
- Mindful meditation: A mental training practice that slows thoughts and calms both mind and body.

- Three-minute breathing: A focus on breath that reduces both stress and anxiety.
- Mindful breathing: An awareness of the present moment without judgment. The emphasis is on one's breath and the mind-body connection.
- Body scan: A systematic focus on different parts of the body that releases physical tension and promotes mental well-being.

A great book to get you started is *Mindfulness: An Eight-Week Plan for Finding Peace in a Frantic World* by Mark Williams and Danny Penman (2012).

For Journaling:

According to several psychologists, certain aspects of our lives are ripe for self-improvement. These include well-being (self-acceptance, personal growth), personality factors (agreeableness, negativity), relationships (marriage, friendships), and achievement (at school or work). These experts agree that we have more success by working on the aspects of our lives proven to be most responsive to change.

To do so, try to carve out about ten minutes of "Me Time" at the end of each week and assess yourself. What did you learn? What do you still need to do? Perhaps respond to these two questions:

- *On a scale of 1 to 10, how would I rate my [self-acceptance, agreeableness, personal growth, etc.] right now?*
- *What do I need to do to raise my ____________ to a ____________?*

Jot some notes in your Notes app, on a spreadsheet, or on several index cards. About every two or three months, review those notes and see where you have grown and where you might still need a little improvement. You will discover that this simple process gives you incentive and direction for a fuller life.

Think About . . .

We don't get old by taking it easy. We get old by continuing to grow. Witness the Gran Abuelo (Great-Grandfather) tree located in Chile's Alerce Costero National Park. It has been growing continuously for 5,484 years (est.). Pretty cool.

Making Mistakes, Handling Criticism

In nature, nothing is perfect and everything is perfect.
Trees can be contorted, bent in weird ways,
and they're still beautiful.
—ALICE WALKER

Ever made a mistake? Ever made a lot of mistakes? Me, too.

Here's one of the realities of life: We're human beings, and as humans we all make mistakes—big mistakes, little mistakes, all kinds of mistakes. They're as inevitable as the sunrise and as persistent as the Andes Mountains in South America. It's impossible to go through life without making at least a couple (maybe even a lot) of mistakes. Count on it!

Here's another reality: The world is quick to criticize and find fault and much slower to praise and find the positive. In other words, when we make mistakes, we are frequently admonished or scolded, but when we do good things, it seems as though we are seldom congratulated. Interestingly, those prone to criticizing others often reveal a lack of success in their own lives. By the same token, those who are happy within themselves need not point out the faults of others. Their happiness often comes from a celebration of others.

Take a look at photographs of the Brazilian grape tree (*Plinia cauliflora*). Here is a tree just ripe for criticism. The purplish-black, white-pulped fruit of this species grows directly on the trunk of the tree—not on any branches. The tree is very slow-growing, and the leaves are often salmon-pink when the tree is young. It tends to prefer acidic soil and needs constant irrigation in order to get sufficient water. In so many respects, this tree does not adhere to all the rules of how a fruit tree should grow or prosper.

It could be easily criticized.

But this tree produces bountiful crops of fruit used in making jams and jellies as well as for eating raw. It is not unusual for a single tree to produce a crop of fruit five or six times during the year. The fruit is one of the most important commercial crops in the central and southern regions of Brazil.

Criticize this tree all you want, but wait until you taste one of the fruits—a taste similar to Muscadine grapes. Yum!

Although criticism is a regular part of day-to-day living, it's how we handle that negativity that makes the difference. The best thing you can do when you're criticized for a mistake is to remember the good in you. Remember your great qualities; remember that you are worthy and that you are capable of good things. Remember that you are still a work in progress, and that you have developed a strong foundation for new experiences and new learnings. Don't fear criticism, but know that when it comes, it's often the result of your successes, not your failures.

By the same token, make a conscious effort to notice the good (not the bad) in others. If someone makes a mistake, let them know in a kind way rather than with derogatory language. In short, praise more than you blame. You'll help others feel better about themselves and you'll feel better about yourself.

Win-win.

In Practice:

Criticism is a form of power. Those who spend their lives criticizing others are trying to assume control over other people's lives. Don't absorb their words. Instead, deflect them, dodge them, or ignore them. Remember, you are the only one in command of your life. Don't allow others to take over that responsibility. Here's a good response whenever someone criticizes you verbally: give them a smile and thank them for their comment. Guess what? You're still in control of you.

For Journaling:

Here's a quote for your consideration: "The best revenge is none. Heal, move on, and don't become like the one who hurt you" (Pamela Short). What do those words say to you? Can you apply them to a recent incident in your life? How could they be important to you going forward? Take a few moments to think about how you might respond to each of those questions. Record your thoughts in a journal and review them every so often. What is the ultimate lesson you would like to take from this?

Think About . . .

Many people consider the Norway maple tree to be one of the messiest trees in the world. In the United States they're invasive, overtaking many native species. However, this tree is completely "unconcerned" about all the criticism. Think about this: A good way to waste a lot of valuable time is to respond to all your critics. Instead, just grow!

Everyone Is Your Teacher

We can learn a lot from trees: they're always grounded, but never stop reaching heavenward.

—EVERETT MAMOR

Several years ago, I wrote a children's book about the ecology of the world's rainforests (*A is for Anaconda: A Rainforest Alphabet*). During my preliminary research, I discovered that one of the most common trees in Central and South American rainforests is the kapok tree—a tree I knew little about. So I consulted two local botanists, attended the rainforest exhibit at the National Aquarium in Baltimore, watched several YouTube videos, and made visits to my local library for resource materials. My explorations revealed some intriguing information.

For example, kapok trees have large, spreading, aboveground roots, known as buttresses, that are large enough to accommodate animals hiding or building their nests. The tree's seed pods contain lightweight, water-resistant fibers used as a filling for life jackets and pillows, as well as for insulating walls. What's more, ancient Mayans embraced the kapok tree as sacred. They believed that souls of the dead would ascend into the branches—a kapok tree can grow to heights of 150 feet or more—which would then allow souls to reach heaven.

The kapok tree's distinguishing characteristics led me into new arenas to learn about rainforests. For almost a year, the kapok was my newfound teacher—an "educator" that helped me discover some intriguing information to share with young readers.

For a moment, let's repurpose the concept of teacher and student, advancing it in a new and quite exciting direction. I'd like you to consider that everyone around you is a potential teacher—a potential expert in an area or field in which you may know little. Consider that every interaction you have with every other human being is a learning opportunity, a way to grow intellectually and emotionally. The individuals you meet and know may not realize they have something to teach, but if you envision every person you meet today as a potential teacher or instructor, you might be surprised at what you learn.

Let's consider some potential teachers:

- The guy who cut you off in traffic was a teacher because he taught you the importance of patience when driving a busy road.
- The man in line at the grocery store who pushed ahead of you in line was a teacher because he taught you why politeness is so important.
- Your best friend who is having serious issues with a significant other was your teacher because she or he taught you the importance of listening.

- Your teenage son who just dyed his hair a brilliant blue was your teacher because he taught you the importance of self-expression without ridicule.
- The car mechanic who overcharged you for a brake job was your teacher because he taught you the importance of getting an estimate before work begins.
- Your spouse who gives you a hug every day when coming home from work is your teacher because he or she taught you the importance of daily affection.
- Your toddler who brushed black India ink all over the dining room wall—and herself—is your teacher because she just taught you the importance of artistic expression. (True story: that creative individual is now a professional artist with a gallery/studio in the north of England, selling her work to an international audience. She also created the painting for the cover of this book.)

When we envision all the people in our lives as teachers, we are less concerned, less annoyed, and less bothered by their actions. Our frustrations diminish exponentially, and a pervasive calmness settles over us. Instead of activating our stress hormones, we change our usual negative reaction to one of positivity and peacefulness. The change is both immediate and enlightening—also educational.

This shift in attitude is a refreshing way of dealing with the slights and injustices of daily living. It takes a little bit of work at first, but when practiced regularly, you will note that your reaction to others makes a dramatic shift. Instead of shouting, "What a jerk!" or "Look what that idiot did," you could discover yourself saying, *Hmmm, I wonder what this person just tried to teach me.*

In Practice:

Ponder all the teachers you might meet today: the young lady who delivers a package to your door, the neighbor who grows beautiful tomatoes, the plumber who fixed a faulty toilet, the teenager who bags your groceries at the supermarket, the clerk at the shoe store, or perhaps you have a teacher or two living right in your own house. What could you learn from each of them? What would you need to do to be more aware of the potential teachers in your life today?

For Journaling:

Pick any day of the week. Make that your Teacher Day. Select one individual (family member, salesperson, restaurant server, fellow driver, next-door neighbor, complete stranger) you encountered during the week—a single individual who served as a teacher for you, either positively or negatively. Record the lesson you learned as a result of that encounter. You may want to maintain a separate journal devoted exclusively to all the lessons you learn over the course of an entire month or year.

Think About . . .

Giant sequoia trees, which often live for three thousand years or more, never stop growing throughout their lives. Keep this in mind: neither are you ever finished; you are always a work in progress.

To Those You Love

In some mysterious way,
woods have never seemed to me to be static things.
In physical terms, I move through them;
yet in metaphysical ones,
they seem to move through me.
—JOHN FOWLES

I stood beside a giant sycamore—one weakened by storms and toppled by wind. It was massive and extraordinary, an impressive timber that radiated beauty and stature. The tree had lived long and flourished, a botanical spectacle that had experienced centuries and, until recently, weathered the storms of life with majesty and dignity. But natural forces had ended its life—changing it from a vertical titan to a horizontal remnant of its once former self. Over long decades it will eventually return to the earth.

I put my hand on its trunk and thanked it for its life, for being part of a grand forest, for bringing joy to visitors, for enriching the soil, for harboring creatures large and small, for producing oxygen, for standing up to climate change, for its eternal beauty.

Too late, I knew, *too late*.

My father passed away less than five weeks after I turned twenty-one. I was on the threshold of adulthood and had lost the opportunity to discuss my dreams and aspirations with him. I never took the time to share some of them while he was alive. Even more significant, I was never able to thank him for the advice and counsel that shaped my life. I couldn't remember if I ever told him, "I love you." For a long time, I felt that an important part of my life was incomplete because I had not expressed my feelings to someone so important to me.

The people in your life deserve to know how they have influenced you, how they have added meaning to your life, and how they are appreciated for sharing their love with you. Waiting for the right time never works because after you're gone, the right time is gone also.

Your eventual passing should not depress you. Use it as motivation for saying what should be said now, not later. Let it provide the impetus to share some of the most important things in life.

Contemplate the following:

1. "I love you." Truth is, we all need to hear those words. They are the ultimate compliment and the ultimate expression of our human connection. Yes, we occasionally say them to spouses and partners, but what about our children, relatives, and dear friends? Love isn't something to be taken for granted; it is something we all like and need to hear. Every. Single. Day.
2. "Thank you." Many people have influenced our life; many people have had a positive effect on who we are and who we are becoming, whatever our age. They have guided our

philosophy and shaped our lives. They have given of themselves, and they deserve our recognition and commendation.

3. "I'm sorry." We all make mistakes; we all sometimes step on someone's toes. That's just the way things are. But not apologizing for our actions is less than human. It diminishes us; it makes us appear uncaring and unsympathetic, and quite frequently, it hurts someone else's feelings. Their day is considerably less than perfect. Say it now. Look them directly in the eyes and say, "I'm sorry." Mean it.
4. "I forgive you." You make mistakes; other people do also. Fact of life: None of us is perfect, yet relationships can be mended with forgiveness; communication can be improved with forgiveness. Forgiveness opens a door that allows us to view what is important in life. Know that forgiveness won't cure everything—but it's a fine start.

Imagine a physician telling you that your life would end in forty-eight hours. What would you want to say to those you love? More important, why are you waiting?

In Practice:

We all have a tendency to ignore the inevitability of our passing. But the truth is that it will happen . . . sometime. Before then, consider all those people who have influenced your life, who have made a difference in who you are, who have given of themselves so that your life is just a little bit better. Sit down and write each of them a thank-you note (a real paper note—not a text or e-mail). They'll appreciate it, and you'll feel much better doing it.

For Journaling:

Are there people in your life who have positively influenced you but are now dead? Take the time to write them a thank-you note, too. You may want to write that note in your journal or in a separate notebook and read it every now and again. Or consider writing that note on a greeting card with no other text and sending it to one of that person's relatives—a daughter, an uncle, a grandparent, a son-in-law. Let them feel the love.

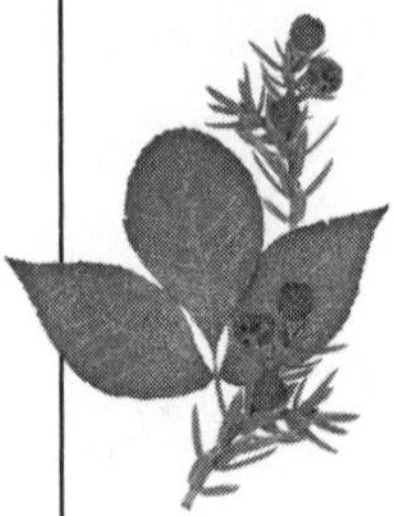

Think About . . .

While walking along the Congress Trail in Sequoia National Park, my mind was filled with rich superlatives and complimentary adjectives. These are trees of magnificence and beacons of longevity. I was in constant admiration. Perhaps one application of the Golden Rule for our daily lives is that people always appreciate being appreciated.

"May I Hold Your Hand?"

When you are lost in the wilderness,
a tree will always point you
in the right direction.
—ANTHONY T. HINCKS

During my tenure as a college professor, I consulted with school districts in various states, presented writing workshops and book talks throughout the country, and delivered keynote addresses and seminars at several education conferences. As a result, I spent a lot of time in airports and on airplanes.

Several years ago, I was flying back home from Chicago to my local airport in Harrisburg, Pennsylvania. I had just completed a daylong author visit in northern Illinois. I boarded the plane and began to settle in for the late-night flight home. Sitting in the window seat next to me was a young woman, about twenty-five years old. She secured her seatbelt and pulled the safety card from the seat pocket in front of her to read several times. Time after time she glanced out the window, and it became obvious that she was extremely nervous. I struck up a conversation, and she told me that she was flying to Pennsylvania to spend some time with her fiancé over the approaching holiday. It was her first time on an airplane.

Closer to flight time, she became more unsettled. The flight attendant reviewed the preflight instructions, and the plane taxied onto the runway. As the engines revved up, she turned and asked me a question I've never forgotten: "I'm really scared. May I hold your hand?"

For the first five minutes of our flight, I held hands with a stranger. As the plane took off, she squeezed my hand with all the resolve of an Olympic wrestler. Prior to our landing she, once again, asked if she could hold my hand, and she did so—fiercely—until the plane taxied up to the gate. As we exited the plane, we continued our conversation, and she thanked me profusely. Later, while retrieving my luggage, I saw her arm in arm with her fiancé. She caught my eye and smiled, and the two of them strolled out of the airport and into the night.

Remember when you were first dating your spouse? Undoubtedly, you spent a lot of time holding hands. Why? Because you were entering a new phase of your life—a phase that may have been a little scary, unknown, and unpredictable. You were learning something new, and hand-holding was a certain way of making it less scary and significantly more enjoyable.

Although I do not make it a practice to hold the hand of the person sitting beside me whenever I fly these days, I try to remember that some passengers may have never flown before. I also try to be aware that some folks have never made pasta carbonara, have never written a children's book, have never crafted a water garden, or have never camped in a wilderness area. One of the best things I can do is to *hold their hands* during the learning process. We may begin the journey as strangers, but we become partners as we reach our destination.

When I walk through a forest, I often focus on the branches of the trees all around. I observe the placement of leaves, the striations of the bark, and the length of their limbs. I also see those branches as arboreal highways for scooting squirrels, creeping caterpillars, dancing songbirds, and inevitable lines of ants searching for food. The branches reach out, extending into cobalt skies or the heart of the forest. They are not human appendages but rather messengers of support and comfort.

I also discover, as I'm walking through a nearby enclave of northern red oaks, chestnut oaks, shagbark hickories, red maples, and tulip poplars, that I am among my best teachers. Perhaps I'm in the beginning stages of crafting a new book—one on a topic I've never pursued. Maybe I'm planning a trip to a country I haven't yet explored. Then again, I might be considering how to help a colleague who's been diagnosed with a disease (Parkinson's) that I've never researched.

This is not anthropomorphism—I'm not seeking to hold hands, outstretched branches—with these trees. Rather, I see those botanical extensions as a sign, a signal, that others might be willing to reach out and assist me in my new journey. While I'm often tempted to go it alone, I realize in my advancing years that challenges are best solved when one embraces the teachers in our lives. A conversation, tall cups of vanilla latte at a local coffee shop, and a large helping of listening with intent can soothe the senses and offer considerable support on the new journey.

I am often reminded of the classic rock song "He Ain't Heavy, He's My Brother" (1969) by the Hollies. If you're not familiar with it, listen to it (and read the lyrics) on YouTube. Then reach out, and hold someone's hand. Even better, allow someone the opportunity to hold your hand and lead you in a new direction. It's certain to be educational.

In Practice:

Here are some common assistance phrases you might want to consider as part of your daily activities:

- "How can I help you?"
- "How may I be of some assistance?"
- "Please allow me to take care of that for you."
- "I'm going to the store. Can I pick up something for you?"
- "Let me hold that for you?"
- "Is there something I can do?"

Is there some time in your day when you might say one of those phrases? Is there some way you can bring a little sunshine into someone's life today? Are you open to being a helping—holding—hand with others?

For Journaling:

Take some time to walk through the quietude of a nearby forest or stretch of woods. Pay particular attention to the outstretched branches all around. Think of them as appendages reaching out to you. Then think about how you might answer any of the following questions:

- What is their message?
- What are they trying to tell me?
- In what ways are they helping me realize a new path or new direction?

Record your thoughts. From time to time revisit those ideas. How might they shape your daily activities?

Think About . . .

Before they slumber for the winter, deciduous trees are ablaze with a riot of blushes, an explosion of pigments, and a plethora of tints. Each night, before you sleep, consider the colors you've shared with the world.

Learning to Breathe

Alone with myself,
the trees bend to caress me.
—CANDY POLGAR

It was early spring, and I was temporarily motionless along the 2.4-mile Boardwalk Loop that winds its way through some of the 26,276 acres of the floodplain forest in Congaree National Park Wilderness—a primeval landscape full of the most magnificent trees eighteen miles south of Columbia, South Carolina. I had come to this humid sanctuary as part of the research necessary for a children's book on swampy environments (*Near One Cattail: Turtles, Logs and Leaping Frogs*). Interestingly, Congaree has one of the largest concentrations of champion trees in the world, with the tallest known examples of fifteen different species—including loblolly pines, American elms, swamp chestnut oaks, and common persimmons. But being tall isn't their only claim to fame. The myriad trees here are part of the largest remaining tract of old-growth bottomland hardwood forests in the United States. Equally significant is that this federally protected forest has the distinction of being an International Biosphere Reserve. In addition, over 80 percent of the park is a federally designated wilderness area.

Strolling the Congaree Boardwalk Loop Trail, I experienced the feeling of being in a Gothic cathedral. The arcing trees hung high overhead as though they were the decorated ceilings of medieval churches in Florence or Assisi. Traipsing beneath these champion trees was a venture through the past, a journey within an arena of longevity and splendor, and an experience that, quite frankly, transcended mere words. Here was a spectacular array of vibrant specimens that underscore the majesty of long-standing trees. Their splendor and their permanence are to be respected as prime examples of nature's wonder—as well as her religion.

Several weeks later, a friend and I were seated in a local Starbucks enjoying some fresh-brewed coffees and discussing literary matters. As a fellow writer, her insights and perceptions about overactive adjectives and the arc of narratives has helped me shape several manuscripts. I had just told her about my trip to Congaree and some of my adventures there. She smiled as I regaled the sights and sounds of my excursions through a regiment of old and lofty trees. She then asked me a most insightful question: "What was the most important thing you learned on your trip?"

I held the coffee cup in my hands, took another sip, and thought about her query for a few moments. I contemplated my explorations of great trees, the timelessness of their existence, the touch of breeze there, and the absence of technological intrusions. Eventually, I looked up and responded, "I learned how to breathe."

Walking through the majestic realm of Congaree—or any forest, for that matter—is both tonic and cathartic. There is a mystical presence, a juxtaposition of calmness and peacefulness that overrides artificial intrusions. In this environment, time—at least the time most familiar to humans—slows perceptibly while sharpening eyesight and focusing the senses. One becomes more attuned to the ebb and flow of the natural world and considerably less focused on the artificiality of electronic messages, crowded calendars, and the constant hum of civilization. This is time as it was—a slow passage of minutes that moves one through an ecosystem and into an inner world. The focus becomes internal—a deeper cognizance of a simple mandate for life: one's breath.

I quickly realized that during the sojourn my pulse had receded, my tension dissipated, my blood pressure dropped, and my awareness of the organicity of life revived. A simple place—a wide and distinguished forest—gave intent for my breath and focus for my journey. Each inhale offered sufficient quantities of O_2 along with a reminder that this was an atmosphere of permanence. Each exhale was a soft and temporary souvenir of a primordial ecosystem, an atmosphere borrowed for a brief trace of time, and an energizing process that certifies one paleo-environment as both authentic and affirming. This is a world where slow breathing is both art and custom, an atmosphere that fills the lungs with possibilities.

My journey through the Congaree grandeur also underscored the Japanese practice of *shinrin-yoku*, or "forest bathing." By definition, forest bathing is simply retreating to a forest environment to experience it through all our senses. It is not an exercise but rather a reconnection with nature through hearing, sight, taste, smell, and touch. It is a more natural and normal existence where we have the opportunity to take in the bend of branches, a flight of migrating birds, the scent of flowered meadows, the taste of a pungent breeze, or a palette of evening colors across the sky. It is an opportunity to reconnect and reorient with a more natural world.

I was sufficiently convinced that this forest had taught me a lesson—the importance of respiration (and quiet contemplation) in a world oversaturated with constant clamor and noise. Breathing the forest is an injection of spirit, an infusion of purpose, and an embrace of deep wonderment into one's being. Each breath fills the lungs with patience and introspection. Forest breathing, I discovered, is a sensual intimacy with beings most grand: an eminent impression of life and personal longevity.

In Practice:

Stand beside a tree or a small cluster of trees. Now breathe, slowly and patiently. What do you feel? Is it the sound of oxygen passing into your lungs or the whoosh of CO_2 moving up your trachea? What sounds familiar, and what is unfamiliar? Is your breath different in the company of trees than in the stress of your work environment?

For Journaling:

Plan a time during the day to focus entirely on your breathing. Start by breathing in gently through your nose while counting from one to five. Then, slowly and calmly, exhale through your nose, again counting from one to five. Do this again and again for at least five minutes. What did you discover or learn? How is this slow and gentle exercise any different from your normal breathing patterns? Take some time and record your thoughts. Perhaps you'd like to create a special breathing journal and record your breathing impressions every week or so.

Think About . . .

Journey through a magnificent forest or deep woods, and you'll notice a prevailing stillness, an overwhelming peace and calmness in the air. As the lyrics of a Simon & Garfunkel song (1964) attest, it is truly the "sound of silence." It is also a reminder that our lives are more beautiful when filled with quiet and tranquility.

How to Walk

Take the power to walk in the forest
and be a part of nature.
—SUSAN POLIS SCHUTZ

You and I and almost every other person on the planet had an epiphany around the time we were two years old. We were all engaged in a task that almost everyone older than two could do with relative ease, but when we tried to do it we failed. Or to use more common vernacular, we flunked—miserably. We were all trying to learn how to walk.

Up until that point in our lives, we had gotten around the house by crawling on our hands and knees—not a very efficient form of locomotion, but practical. Our bodies had not yet developed the strength or balance to stand on both feet without falling over. But we saw that everyone else in the family was walking on two feet, and it seemed only logical that we should. So we tried to stand up. And we fell down—not once or twice, but many times. Day after day, week after week, we would try to stand up, and we would always fall down.

But we kept trying, and through sheer determination and persistence we learned to walk. Tentative steps at first, then wobbly steps, then steps with more assurance and confidence. After a couple of weeks, we were officially *walkers*. We had used our failures as learning opportunities. We pushed through all the times our butts made contact with the living room floor and learned how to walk on our own. We had turned failure into success. Our growth mindset was firmly in place.

But then we grew up and something happened, as though an invisible switch were flipped in our heads. We discarded failure as a learning tool and saw it as something to be avoided. For many of us, this change may have come about as a result of enduring lots of criticism during our formative years. Because we experienced humiliation or shame throughout our childhoods ("Why can't you be an A student like your brother?"), we carry those feelings into adulthood and avoid tasks that might have unsuccessful results. By avoiding any chance of failure, we believe we can also avoid any chance of being ridiculed or denounced.

As a result, we often tag ourselves with a label that frequently achieves a sense of permanency—*I have failed a lot, thus I must be a failure.* What we often forget is that failures are an inevitability of everyday living; they are not a life sentence. Self-designating ourselves as a *failure* over time develops into a mental block that is difficult to override. It becomes a mantra we often embrace whenever faced with any type of challenge.

A predominant evergreen throughout Arizona, New Mexico, and western Texas, the redberry juniper is a small tree often topping out at twenty feet or less. It can be found on grasslands and rocky slopes, and coyotes, birds, foxes, racoons, jackrabbits, and other small mammals consume its berries. It survives in an ecologically challenging environment dictated by high temperatures and a dearth of water.

This tree is also distinctive because it can resprout from its stump after burning, cutting, or shredding. This resprouting characteristic makes it one of the most difficult plants to control and manage. Even more important, the tree has dealt with environmental failure by evolving to take advantage of an extensive root system and abundant food reserves so that it can rise up once again. As for a child learning to walk, failure is simply an incentive to move in a new direction.

Several psychologists have put forward the notion that although most of us hate to fail, for some of us failing presents an overwhelming psychological threat such that our motivation to avoid failure often exceeds our motivation to succeed. This fear causes us to unconsciously sabotage our chance of success. As others contend, humans often do more to avoid pain than they do to gain pleasure.

Experts have also pointed out that for many people it is not the actual failure that elicits the fear, but rather that a fear of failure is essentially a fear of shame. By this definition, a fear of failure means we are motivated to avoid a potentially uncomfortable experience—not because we can't manage the basic emotions of disappointment and frustration, but more because failing induces more intense feelings of embarrassment, humiliation, or remorse. Failing is often seen as a weakness or a public display of several weaknesses. And when those weaknesses are revealed, our self-worth suffers mightily.

The key is to see failure as inevitable—a normal and natural occurrence of everyday life. It is not a death sentence but rather an opportunity to learn something new. It's a chance to move in new directions and discover new information. This realization alone is a refreshing way to approach each day. In so doing, we give ourselves permission to stumble a little (like a youngster learning to walk) but also incentive to profit from the experience. We discover greater satisfaction, a more confident self-concept, and a renewed spirit of adventure.

Just like we did as children.

In Practice:

Here are some statements for your review. Select one, write it on an index card or Post-it note, and place it on your desk.

- Failing is part of the learning process, rather than the end of a project or challenge.
- Acknowledge, accept, and celebrate your imperfections. They make you unique.
- Effort is more important than talent. Reward your hard work, not your final product.
- Take a risk; take a chance. Try new things just because . . . just because they're new—not because they're safe.
- Don't aim for perfection; rather, aim for the learning that's involved. Far better to be a constant learner than a person who rests on one's laurels.
- If you are wrestling with a challenge or struggling with a problem, tell yourself that you haven't quite mastered it *yet*. Perseverance is just as important as effort.

For Journaling:

Consider the following quotes and not only how they might impact your concept of failure but also how they might contribute to your successes. Take some time and record your thoughts in a journal.

- "People succeed when they realize that their failures are the preparation for their victories." —Ralph Waldo Emerson
- "Success is the ability to go from failure to failure without losing your enthusiasm." —Winston Churchill
- "My great concern is not whether you have failed, but whether you are content with failure." —Abraham Lincoln
- "Our greatest glory is not in never failing, but in rising every time we fail." —Confucius
- "It is fine to celebrate success, but it is more important to heed the lessons of failure." —Bill Gates
- "If you're not failing, you're not growing." —H. Stanley Judd
- "Remember that failure is an event, not a person." —Zig Ziglar (one of my favorites)

Think About . . .

Red maple trees release thousands of seeds that fall to the ground. As a result, seeds are dispersed over a wide area—many of them eventually germinating. In human terms, no child ever learned how to walk without falling down. Give yourself permission to fall down every now and again. Something wonderful may germinate as a result.

Part III

Bark Up the Right Tree

A Community of Roots

Learn character from trees, values from roots,
and change from leaves.
—TASNEEM HAMEED

We owned the trail. No chattering children. No teenagers with blaring radios. No bands of misguided adults talking over the quiet. There was solemnity all around—the way of the forest predominated as it should.

We were on a venture through the majesty of redwoods. Our steps, slow and measured, were intentional. We took in as much as our eyes could hold and created rich visions in our minds that would last for decades. On this journey we ambled along a well-maintained trail in Prairie Creek Redwoods State Park. Clouds scuttled overhead as we wove our way among some of the most majestic beings on the planet. They were sentinels of time, masters of arboreal beauty. The quiet, occasionally broken by a distant bird's call or the creaking of two side-by-side trees rubbing against each other in the breeze, was pervasive.

On occasion, we would step over thick roots protruding from the soil—haphazardly weaving their way across the trail or around tall timbers. Redwood roots are both their lifeblood as well as their strength. Amazingly, for trees so massive and tall, the roots seldom penetrate the earth more than five or six feet. The lack of depth is made up by their length, with roots often extending up to a hundred feet or more away from the trunk. As redwoods rise in massive groves, those roots often tangle and intertwine as would happen when a skein of yarn is attacked by a rambunctious cat left alone for an entire day.

Not only do those roots hold massive trees in place and obtain sustenance for their continual growth, but they also stand against substantial storms, long-term erosion, and thunderous coastal winds. This is their strength against the constant forces of nature. Beyond the embrace of roots, the potency of redwoods is in their interactions with one another—the sharing of life-sustaining resources and the cellular lines of communication with which they pass along vital data about the infestation of insects or the approach of fire.

In my passing through this enclave, I was reminded of our own need for communities, our own need for support and sustenance from others. Rarely do redwoods exist in isolation; they are typically community-minded timbers—clusters of individuals (sometimes referred to as fairy circles or fairy rings) as well as immense groves of trees in a limited area. It would be safe to say that redwoods need one another for safety, sustenance, and, unsurprisingly, strength.

As do we.

While we often identify ourselves as individuals, we cannot survive in isolation. Sure, we need time and place for personal thoughts and contemplation, but that time is occasional. Our growth and maturation are, quite often, dependent on family, friends, and neighbors who offer support, counsel, and simple companionship. They share their own strength, assist us with life's problems or challenges, and hold our hand in times of turmoil or conflict. These people are necessary for our spiritual health and emotional stability. We thrive in their company; we grow in their presence. When with others, we are redwoods.

You most likely enjoy deep conversations with friends—discussions about life, politics, movies, travel, and new experiences. There is personal reflection in words shared, intellectual challenges in positions taken or thoughts changed. You are nourished in so many ways by the company of others: your spirit is renewed, your vision sharpened, and your life strengthened.

In his book *The Blue Zones: 9 Lessons for Living Longer from the People Who've Lived the Longest* (2012), author Dan Buettner notes that one of the most significant factors contributing to a long life (living into one's eighties, nineties, and beyond) is membership in a supportive community. Buettner presents compelling research demonstrating that community membership adds four to fourteen years to human life expectancy. Groups, it seems, contribute mightily to one's longevity, whether one is a tree or *Homo sapiens.*

A commingling of roots gave me pause in my contemplation of arboreal teachings. It taught me that our foundation as a species is, most certainly, one of many individuals in support of one another.

Think about this: like redwoods, we grow best in the company of others.

In Practice:

If you haven't done so already, consider joining a group that promotes a cause you believe in, that helps others who may be less fortunate than you, or that just needs a little money every now and then to carry out their mission. It could be a national organization (the Sierra Club, Salvation Army, Heifer International) or something more local (a regional housing project, a local food bank, an organization that supports high school athletic teams). Know that giving to others is also giving to ourselves.

For Journaling:

Walk through a nearby forest or wooded hillside. Carry your journal with you and occasionally record your response(s) to one or more of the following queries:

- What are some of the strengths of that ecosystem?
- How are the trees supporting one another?
- Are the trees more beautiful when together or when standing apart?
- If you were a tree, where would you like to stand in that assembly?

Now, consider a group or organization you are part of.

- How is that group similar to a forest of trees?
- How do members support one another?
- How do they share their philosophies or views on life?
- What contributes to their cohesiveness?
- What makes the group strong (or not)?

Any similarities? Any connections?

Think About . . .

Remember: The good life is seldom a solo effort. Aspen trees form extensive groves with a vast interconnected root system. One assembly of 47,000 aspens in south central Utah has lived for more than 9,000 years. Surround yourself with supportive friends. They help you grow old, too.

A Curious Life

Between every two pines
is a doorway to a new world.
—JOHN MUIR

As naturally inquisitive creatures, we are fascinated with the unknown, we are transfixed with the mysteries of life that surround us, and we are amazed at all that we have to explore. The mysteries of the world around have always been an impetus for us to peek and poke and prod for answers—learning something about our surroundings as well as about ourselves. Nowhere is this truer than when we watch the youngest among us—our children.

Children are known for sticking their fingers in places where they should never be. They are famous for putting all manner of objects and substances in their mouths—everything from plastic blocks, the dog's ears, and any object in the room not nailed down or sufficiently weighted. As any parent knows, after learning to walk, children will expand their curiosity by reading new books, looking under rocks, or creating music with pots, pans, and other kitchen utensils. Theirs is a world full of unknowns propelled by a desire to discover and learn.

Young children are often described as very curious creatures—always exploring new territories and new opportunities. Just like the roots of pinyon pines.

Pinyon pines typically inhabit broad areas of the American Southwest. They are often known for their production of pinyon nuts—an edible food of Native Americans and a staple of southwestern cuisine for generations. But perhaps pinyon pines' most distinctive feature is their wide-spreading roots.

Pinyon pines live in a harsh and demanding environment: arid conditions, fierce winds, and rocky substrates. In order to obtain necessary water, the roots of this tree seek out and penetrate the minutest of fissures or cracks in surrounding rocks. They sneak their way into the smallest of crevices, patiently inching their way toward any available water or nutrients. They create a conglomerate of tiny rootlings that split, weave, and wind their way through minuscule rocks and immense boulders. Not only does this ensure adequate resources for the tree, but it also provides a root system that acts as an anchor in its demanding geography.

In anthropomorphic terms, pinyon pines are curious. Their roots peek and poke through the earth in a constant search for nourishment and viability. It is as though they were inquiring, wanting to discover something new, exciting, and of sustenance. That curiosity keeps them alive, sustaining their being.

For many of us, curiosity guides us toward a lifetime occupation, drives us to search out potential mates, and stimulates us to travel to new destinations. But, then, something happens. As we age, we tend to lose our sense of curiosity. We begin to believe that as we grow older, we grow smarter. (The Pennsylvania Dutch put it this way: "We grow too soon old and too late smart.") Then we get to a point in our lives when we think we know it all. We've had certain experiences, talked with numerous people, read a variety of books, traveled to many places, and accumulated a lot of information.

Been there, done that.

However, one thing consistently injects or reinjects spirit into our lives, no matter our age: the full embrace of our natural curiosity as humans—the same level of curiosity we enjoyed as children. This involves actively seeking new destinations, engaging with new people, and most important, asking new questions. It's a commitment to know more than we know; to expand our horizons, try out the new and undiscovered; and pursue experiences that deepen our comprehension and appreciation of the world. It's a constant revitalization of life, an embrace of the unknown.

Think of it this way: Curiosity generates possibilities. When we look at the world from multiple perspectives, we give ourselves permission to examine a wider range of personal resolutions and individual remedies.

In Practice:

Here are several strategies proven to enhance your curiosity. Inject one or more of these into your daily activities:

- **Ask more questions in conversations.** Tap into the background knowledge of others to improve your own. Dig deep, explore further.
- **Travel widely.** Seek out new places, new cultures, new

viewpoints. Travel opens your eyes to new ways of thinking and new ways of experiencing the world.

- **Read outside your experience.** Expand your reading horizons; read from several different genres. The best books to read are those about subjects you never studied in school.
- **Hang out with curious people.** Curious folks are models for us all; they give us personal examples to emulate, an opportunity to see "curiosity" as a verb.
- **Question yourself.** Don't make the assumption that everything you learned in school is all you need to know in life. In short, question everything you ever learned. Refresh regularly.
- **Talk with different people.** Branch out from your usual friends and associates. Every personal encounter gives you an opportunity to learn something new.
- **Walk in nature.** Time in nature ignites our curiosity. When your curiosity batteries are on low, a walk in the woods is the surest way to recharge.
- **Be interested in everything.** Move out and beyond your comfort zone. Examine the unexamined, explore the unexplored, and investigate the uninvestigated. The wider your reach, the more expansive your discoveries.

For Journaling:

Start each day with a question. Ask yourself a question regarding a topic or subject about which you know little. For example,

- "Why do people get shorter as they get older?"
- "Why are oceans so salty?"
- "What is the only state that does not have a straight line in its border?"

- "Who was the tallest human who ever lived?"
- "How do trees create oxygen?"
- "What the heck is pi?"

Spend some time discovering the answers. Sure, use the Internet, but also consider asking friends, checking out a book at your local library, or inquiring at a local college. Make question-asking one of your daily priorities, and you may discover that some interesting things happen in your future.

Think About . . .

Willow trees often have root systems that spread three to four times the height of the tree, always seeking nourishment. This reminds me that I'd rather be with someone still curious, still reaching out, than someone who has all the answers.

Rejecting Rejection

Be like a tree. The tree gives shade
to him who cuts off its boughs.
—SRI CHAITNYA

Ever been rejected? Yeah, me, too. The server at the local diner never returned your smile. Rejection! Somebody said something unkind about your new hairstyle. Rejection! You made a creative suggestion at work, and someone said, "Give me a break. That'll never work!" Rejection! You're a writer, and your latest article was just turned down. Rejection!

Rejection is everywhere. Sometimes it seems as though everyone is rejecting our ideas, our style, our opinions, and our way of life. Obviously, we don't like to be rejected. We don't like to be told that our ideas or beliefs aren't worth anything. Aside from the expected blow to our emotions, there's evidence to suggest that we suffer physiologically as well. For example, when a coworker says that she doesn't think your idea is a good one, there is a sudden release throughout your body of dozens of stress-producing hormones. These chemicals have a decided impact on your brain, sufficient to result in an impairment of logic and reasoning as well as your ability to communicate and use language.

Now consider the lowly mulberry tree. Most people reject these trees for one simple reason—they are incredibly messy. A single tree produces a large number of berries, and when those berries mature, they fall from the tree. They fall on houses; sidewalks, streets, and cars; decks and outdoor furniture; and people. Quite often these fruits stain whatever they fall on—a stain difficult to wash away. Mulberry trees are hated—or rejected—because of their unpleasantness.

But mulberries, in spite of their messiness, are also celebrated as a delicious food—most notably in pies, tarts, wines, and herbal teas. So, too, have they become part of our literary heritage ("Here We Go 'Round the Mulberry Bush") as well in art (one of Vincent van Gogh's most notable paintings is *Mulberry Tree* [1889]). It seems as though the mulberry tree, in spite of its constant rejections, has done quite well as a botanical icon.

A wonderful strategy for dealing with the constant onslaught of rejection is to accept it as a part of everyday life. Know that rejection is inevitable—it is often a way people try to establish their superiority, to prove that they know better than you what is right and what is wrong. Instead of letting rejection sink beneath your skin, allow it to bounce away. It's a distraction—someone's way of diminishing your worth without your permission.

In short, reject rejection.

One of the classic examples of literary rejection is Dr. Seuss's first book: *And to Think That I Saw It on Mulberry Street* (note the title)—one that received twenty-seven rejections from twenty-seven different publishers before Vanguard Press accepted it in 1937. But it was a book he truly believed in, so he kept his focus on the ultimate goal: publication. He persevered, and because of his perseverance and his belief in his work, the domain of children's literature was changed forever.

In that same vein, *Gone with the Wind* by Margaret Mitchell was initially rejected by thirty-eight publishers; *Carrie* by Stephen King (his first book) was rejected thirty times before it was eventually published; *Harry Potter and the Sorcerer's Stone* by J. K. Rowling was rejected eight times; *Dune* by Frank Herbert was rejected by twenty-three publishing houses; and John Grisham's first book, *A Time to Kill*, was turned down by sixteen different publishers. By the way, the book you are now holding in your hands was initially rejected by fourteen different publishers before HCI Books accepted it.

My motto: "Rejection is just one person's opinion; it is not an obituary."

In Practice:

Rejection happens all the time—in our family lives, our work environments, our romantic encounters, and our day-to-day encounters with others. Embrace the following principles, and develop a healthier attitude about rejection:

- Rejection is inevitable. Everyone experiences it at various times in their lives.
- The best way to deal with rejection is to not take it personally. One act of rejection is not a condemnation of your entire life.
- Constantly remind yourself of your value. You are still an important person.
- Not everyone agrees with you. Not everyone sees the world as you do. And that's okay.
- Don't fall into the trap of blaming yourself. Keep your head high.
- Most important, know that rejection is a temporary judgment—quite often an opinion that will, soon enough, be "gone with the wind."

For Journaling:

Everybody gets rejected some time during their life—often, many times! Rejection, remember, has nothing to do with your personal worth or your inner being—it is merely an event, not who you are. Take some time to deal with the inevitable rejections of life by reframing them. For example, write down a recent "rejection" such as "She didn't like my new dress." After that statement, write something positive, such as "Someone else will certainly like it as much as I do." Here are some other examples:

(A) "Alice told me I had a bad temper yesterday."

(B) "Sometimes I have bad days, but most of the time I'm really a happy camper."

(A) "The guy in the truck swore at me when I cut in front of him."

(B) "Yes, I made a mistake. But that's not me. I'm normally very careful and considerate when I drive."

(A) "My new book was turned down by fourteen publishers."

(B) "I can't wait to hear how excited the next publisher will be when they see my work!"

Think About . . .

Silver maple trees have a root system that tears up yards, clogs water lines, and breaks up sidewalks. Native Americans, on the other hand, used the sap of silver maples to make sugar, medicine, and bread. Like a wise philosopher said, "Keep in mind that it is your thinking that is negative, not your life."

The Power of Play

Keep a green tree
in your heart and perhaps a
singing bird will come.
—CHINESE PROVERB

I'd like to invite you to go to a local playground or public park and spend some time watching children at play. They may be running, jumping, doing cartwheels, playing tag, barreling down a slide, climbing a jungle gym, or tossing a Frisbee. The air most likely will be filled with their laughter, shouts, excitement, and lots of joy. Now, a question:

How much play is in your life or in your day?

We often have the mistaken idea that play is the sole province of children, seldom adults. So, too, do we believe that playtime is nonproductive time—life without rules or structure. Yet a convincing body of psychological research shows that adults—just like children—need sufficient playtime opportunities to achieve balance and perspective in their lives. Compelling research also suggests that children smile about twenty times a day more than adults and laugh ten times a day more than adults do.

Hmmm, must be all that play!

A few years ago I was doing some book research along the Olympic Peninsula of Washington State. I flew into Seattle, drove south on Interstate 6 through Tacoma and past Olympia, then north on Highway 101 as it ribbons its way up the peninsula. A dark bank of clouds, the parting remnants of the previous night's rainstorm, scudded across the horizon. Sunlight forced its way around the edges, accenting the late morning landscape. A corridor of western red cedar, Sitka spruce, Douglas fir, and bigleaf maples enveloped me on both sides of the highway. A breeze blew in from the ocean, causing leaves to dance and twirl in the dappled sunshine.

I pulled off the road and watched closely. I saw leaves moving as in a symphony. Each was a tiny dancer, a ballet of measured movements upon the lightest breeze. In unison, they conjured up images of grace upon the stage: Misty Copeland, Mikhail Baryshnikov, Twyla Tharp, Rudolf Nureyev—dancers who linger in our minds long after their performances are finished or careers complete. Their style and substance are polished works of art: flair and elegance; timeless beauty. So, too, the leaves.

The leaves were reminders that there is joy in action, life in play. The average adult sits for an average of six and one-half hours a day (American adolescents spend eight and a quarter hours per day sitting). Our days, often commanded by sedentary habits, become the same-old, same-old. Without rhythm or engagement.

Time to get up and gambol with the wind. Like children, be playful; move with zephyrs, laugh with the sun, smile at the day—pirouette, sauté, plié. Your tension and stress will dissipate, your joy will escalate. You'll rekindle the spontaneity of life and rediscover the passion of childhood. You'll reroute your emotions and refresh your attitude. You'll embrace the wind and celebrate the day. You'll change from sedentary to passionate.

Take time to dance like leaves. They know!

In Practice:

Play is often defined as doing something you enjoy with no real purpose or specific agenda. You don't even need to be good at it; it just needs to be pleasurable. Watch kids trying to climb up a sliding board at the local park or play a game of tag at the beach, and you have a good idea of play. Play is equally important for adults because it helps them cope with stress, enhances relaxation, promotes creativity, mitigates anxiety, and promotes general well-being. Inserted into your everyday activities it can have a positive impact on your attitudes and emotions. Here are a few playful suggestions: adult coloring books, tossing a ball back and forth, a game of cornhole or horseshoes at the local park, arcade games, playing tennis, doing crosswords or playing solitaire on your cell phone or tablet, jigsaw puzzles, collecting things, jogging, photography, making candles, wood craft, jewelry making, pickleball, board games, trivia quizzes, digital drawing, and scrapbooks are all possibilities. Consider the well-worn saying "All work and no play make Jack a dull boy." Adults, too.

For Journaling:

Recent research demonstrates that there are three general benefits of play: (1) positively coping with stress, (2) boosting your overall physical health, and (3) enhancing your overall well-being. After engaging in a daily or regular playtime activity, record how it impacted your level of stress, your physical health, or your general well-being. In what ways did you change or improve? How did your mood improve? What might be some of the long-term implications of more play in your life?

Think About . . .

The wind blows and the leaves of ginkgo trees shimmy and shutter, wobble and wiggle, quiver and quake. A joyful dance against a turquoise sky. Ginkgos have been around for more than 290 million years. Must have something to do with all that play.

Managing Stress

But I'll tell you what hermits realize.
If you go off into a far,
far forest and get very quiet,
you'll come to understand that you're
connected with everything.

—ALAN WATTS

A teacher friend has an amazing outlook on life. Always happy, always content, she is the epitome of the self-actualized woman. She has a kind word for everyone she works with, and she models joy and energy with her students throughout the school year. She is, in many ways, a consummate teacher and an excellent human being.

In a conversation I had with her, she shared an important lesson, one she learned many years ago. Like most teachers, she has plenty of stress in her life, and she is willing to accept that. But what she related about how she handles that stress made the most sense. She says that her definition of stress management is not just what she does for herself (internal) but also what she does for others (external). For example, she rewards herself with an occasional short note about an important task she completed and how well she did it. In addition, she takes a few minutes to write a colleague a complimentary note about all the planning that went into the school's science fair. She takes time from her busy schedule to indulge herself in a massage at the local health club. At the same time, she makes a point to hug each of her first-grade students when they arrive in the morning. (Psychologists tell us that there are several benefits to hugging, irrespective of age, including a reduction in stress and sickness, a boost in heart health, an increase in happiness, a reduction of pains and fears, as well as better communication.)

Bromeliads are plants that grow in the understory and canopy layers of the rainforest—particularly on the branches of many rainforest trees. Although they do not have roots, they have developed a unique way of obtaining necessary water and nutrients. Most have curved leaves that overlap at the base—forming a tight bowl at the bottom. The leaves act like a gutter to collect falling rain, and the tank holds the water. In a way, they have evolved to deal with one of the stressors of treetop living.

They also give back to their environment by providing a home to many varieties of rainforest animals, including frogs, insects, worms, and spiders. Scientists have discovered more than 250 varieties of animals in the tanks of bromeliads. In turn, the animals leave their droppings in the tanks, providing nourishment to the plants. When these animals die, their bodies also contribute to the plants' growth. This interaction between different species is known as "mutualism"—the ecological interaction between two or more species where each species has a net benefit.

For my friend, stress management is all about mutualism—all

about balance. She knows she will never eliminate the stress in her life, but she believes that she can better manage stress because she takes care of herself *and* takes care of the people in her life. Her stress management plan is one in which she and others are all participants.

Achieving balance in our lives is not easy; it takes work. However, when we give to others *and* give to ourselves, we can make a difference in our lives and in the lives of those around us. This is stress management at its finest.

In Practice:

When you wake up in the morning, set a goal of identifying one person in your life for whom you can alleviate an issue, a problem, or a concern. Perhaps it's a child who struggles with math, a spouse facing a major decision at work, a friend who's dealing with a serious medical condition, or a senior citizen just looking for someone to talk to. Make this a daily or regular practice, and you may discover that some of the stressors in your life are significantly reduced also.

For Journaling:

Hand-write a letter or a note (not an e-mail or text) to someone who is dealing with an issue or predicament in their life. Offer comfort and compassion in your message. What would they like to hear (what would you like to hear if in the same situation)? What would alleviate some of their negative feelings or emotions? How do you think they might react if you shared this essay with them?

Think About . . .

The roots of a mesquite tree grow laterally about forty-five feet away from the trunk. Like a mesquite, perhaps we should spend more time reaching out, less time standing still.

Talking with Ourselves

A lion chased me up a tree,
and I greatly enjoyed the view from the top.
—CONFUCIUS

How often do you engage in negative self-talk? For many of us, that happens far too often. We have this inner dialogue telling ourselves that we are not successful, we are not doing the work that needs to be done, or that we have far too many imperfections. We often believe that these conversations will help incentivize us to rise above adversities or challenges. We think we are motivating ourselves, but we're doing the opposite. We're creating a self-fulfilling prophecy.

We're validating our negative thoughts, giving them more credence than they deserve. We're in a funk and will, most likely, stay in that funk for some time.

For the moment, I'd like to invite you to consider tree seeds. Each year, depending on the species, trees will disperse anywhere from dozens to hundreds of thousands of seeds. Where those seeds land

and whether they will ultimately germinate is due to a wide variety of factors, internal (e.g., the shape of the seed) and external (e.g., specific soil nutrients). That said, I'd like to anthropomorphize a single seed from a single tree. That is, I'd like to give that seed a voice and ask you to imagine it is having a conversation with itself as it falls to the ground.

Here is what it might say, "I sure hope I land on fertile ground, but the wind is really blowing hard today, and I'll probably land in some desert area with no water. Or with my luck, I'll probably fall near a hungry chipmunk who will gobble me up for her dinner. Or maybe I'll land on a busy highway and be crushed by an eighteen-wheeler. Chances are I'll fall in someone's yard and be mowed into oblivion. Oh, woe is me!"

That is one anxious seed!

But we often do the same thing to ourselves. One of the strategies I use whenever I find myself falling into some negative self-talk is to create a negative/positive statement. Here's how it works: Write down a sentence that begins with a negative thought but ends with a positive thought. Here are some examples:

- "I didn't get everything done in the garden today, but I was able to get a beautiful row of hostas planted in the front of the house."
- "I wasn't able to finish chapter 3 in the book I'm writing, but I did create a terrific introduction that will impress my editor."
- "I don't think my new colleague likes my office decorations, but I can't wait for the neighborhood block party this coming weekend."
- "I was sorta grouchy with my sister when she called, but I'll write her a note expressing my gratitude for thinking about me."

What happens with this strategy is that you break the continuous cycle of negative talk with something positive. Instead of replaying negativity repeatedly, you begin to shift your thoughts in a different (positive) direction.

Our mythical talking seed might utter something like "The ground is really dry around here, but I'm strong and should be able to survive for a few days until it rains."

The thoughts that circulate through our heads are just that: thoughts. By recognizing and identifying those ideas as immaterial reflections (rather than concrete entities), we alter our relationship to those thoughts. We begin to realize that we're having a thought that, in most cases, doesn't have to be true. When we counter those thoughts with a negative/positive statement, we put them in their proper place. In so doing, we reward ourselves with a more positive attitude and outlook and develop a deeply loving relationship with ourselves.

In Practice:

Psychologists suggest that we engage in positive self-talk on a regular basis. Consider some of the following tips:

- Be aware of times when you talk negatively about yourself.
- Take time, every so often, to check in with your feelings.
- Seek out and surround yourself with positive friends, colleagues, and family members.
- Include humor in your life. Listen to podcasts that make you laugh, watch humorous movies, read funny books, collect jokes.
- Give yourself one positive affirmation every single day. Every. Single. Day.

For Journaling:

Keep a journal or notebook on your desk or in a location at home that you use frequently. At the end of each day write down a negative/positive statement about an event, circumstance, or situation that occurred during the day. Occasionally evaluate those statements. How helpful are they in reducing the amount of negative self-talk?

You may want to keep track of the number of negative statements you say about yourself during the day in relation to the number of positive things. How might you pair one of those negative statements with one of the positive statements? Write down your creation and consider sharing it with a friend or relative.

Think About . . .

On average, a tree will have approximately 200,000 leaves—most healthy and vibrant, others not so much. On average, each human being has about 50,000 thoughts a day. It's up to you to decide how many of those thoughts are positive or negative.

Responsible You

Storms make trees take
deeper roots.
—DOLLY PARTON

Are you responsible? Many adults answer yes to that question, because they are aware of the necessary responsibilities of a job, maintaining a home, raising children, and supporting friends. You attend to those necessary tasks faithfully and without question. Right?

Let me ask that question another way. Do you accept responsibility for yourself? You might be inclined to answer that question in the affirmative simply because you live with yourself at first, and then you live with others. You take care of yourself physically and mentally, and you feel pretty good about who you are and what you are doing in life. Of course, you are responsible for yourself.

I would like to suggest yet another perspective on this question. Psychologists state that people need to spend more time resolving, rather than enduring, personal problems. We often spend more time and effort resolving the difficulties and challenges of others when we should take the time to address our own personal problems. I agree with this thesis, but I also see another point of view.

We do not grow as loving and committed human beings unless we take charge of our own lives. You and I and a few billion other people in the world face challenges and difficulties daily. The difference is how we perceive them. Are we willing to accept the shortcomings and deficiencies in our lives? Do we endure our imperfections and dog paddle our way through life? Are we content with our personal status quo?

Conversely, are we willing to put ourselves in charge of our self-improvement? The resolution of a problem is usually not evolutionary; it requires determination and action. It requires someone to take the initiative and to take charge. Time alone does not solve problems; they are solved because someone decides to take action.

There is a tree, the Shajarat-al-Hayat, that stands alone in a barren area of the Arabian Desert. It is a solitary tree—no plants around for miles—that has anchored itself in this arid environment for more than four hundred years. It has endured temperatures that often reach more than 110 degrees along with an average annual rainfall of less than three inches. But it has continued to exist for more than four centuries.

Legend has it that the tree is protected by the God of Water, Enki. However, scientists have determined that the tree's roots are at least 164 feet long—allowing the tree to reach deep into the earth to obtain groundwater. From an evolutionary standpoint, this tree has taken charge of its own life; faced with harsh environmental conditions, it sought relief and resolution by extending itself deeper into the ground for a vital resource. It survives—quite well—because it took necessary action on its own. For that reason, the Shajarat-al-Hayat is often referred to as the "Tree of Life."

The great mystery is why no other trees have been able to tap into this deep-earth resource, this wellspring of life.

I am the best person to solve my problems or improve my imperfections. Certainly, I take counsel from friends and family, and I read the advice of experts and counselors. Ultimately, though, I am the one who makes the decision or takes the action. I am responsible for me.

Are you responsible for you?

In Practice:

One of the themes woven throughout this book is the value of time spent among trees or in forests as one of the most positive activities we can do to take care of ourselves. Dynamic and convincing research suggests that time in nature significantly reduces our stress, helps us sleep better, positively alters our mood, lowers our blood pressure, reduces our fatigue, and helps us overcome symptoms of depression. A regular walk in the company of trees may be the best thing we can do for ourselves in terms of mental health, contentment, and personal rejuvenation.

How about a walk in the woods today?

For Journaling:

One of the best ways to practice self-care is to learn how to say no. Admittedly, it's a challenge for many people. When we commit ourselves to helping others, we often discover that we are saying yes more often and to more people. Saying no is a most difficult skill, particularly when others ask for our input or assistance. But, as you can imagine, too many yeses can lead to burnout and additional stressors in our lives. Saying no takes a lot of practice, but it can result in more time for our own growth and development. Every so often, take a few moments and record a time when you wanted to say no, but actually said yes. Why was that difficult? What might be another way to respond?

Think About . . .

The tropical wiliwili tree lives solely in Hawai'i, nowhere else in the world—an environmental choice. Go ahead, choose your own attitude for today. Don't allow others to choose it for you. You'll grow taller.

Acts of Kindness

A single act of kindness
throws out roots in all directions,
and the roots spring up and make new trees.
—AMELIA EARHART

When I go into my credit union to deposit a check or take out some money, I'll engage the teller in a brief conversation, "Hey, April, looks like a busy day here. How are you doing?" And we'll have a short conversation. When I go into a retail store to purchase a new shirt or a gift certificate for my wife, I'll make a point to talk with the clerk. "Hi, how's business today?" A few sentences will be exchanged, and I'll complete my purchase and make a comment like "Thanks for the conversation. Hope you have a great day."

I've always believed in the concept of random acts of kindness. A smile, a comment, a brief conversation takes little time but always brings great rewards—particularly for the recipient(s). For me, conversation is an effective way of communicating respect without expecting anything in return. It's a way of celebrating a service I wouldn't be able to complete on my own, recognizing that someone employed to do so is taking care of my needs. They certainly deserve something more than a grumble, complaint, or gripe. They deserve my recognition.

Several years ago, I was invited to make a keynote speech in New Orleans. Phyllis accompanied me, and we decided to add a few extra days onto the schedule. One of our planned activities was a tour of various neighborhoods throughout the city, including the Garden District, Uptown, and Mid-City. Here and there we came across several magnificent crape myrtle trees—each decorated with pink, purple, white, lavender, or red blooms. It was mid-June, and the trees dazzled with their picturesque branches, symmetrical shapes, and profusion of beauty—whether in private backyards or near commercial enterprises. Each encounter was one that required a photograph or two, or at least a momentary pause to admire their splendor.

I recognized that these delightful trees had given us something—something we neither asked for nor demanded. Just as they had shared their beauty with residents of the city, so, too, had they injected a note of beauty into our lives, without any expectation. Their giving was part and parcel of their natural beauty. I didn't demand their attention, but their attention was given nonetheless. I remember those images to this day.

Committing random acts of kindness brings enormous contentment into your life. Not only will it reward you with positive feelings, but it also rewards the recipient with recognition and appreciation that are seldom shared. A few words exchanged with friends and strangers can make all the difference in the world. More often than not, it results in a smile, satisfaction, and renewed energy for the giver as well as the recipient.

If you're looking for kindness activities to share with others (including people you know and those you've never met), check out the Random Acts of Kindness Foundation (www.randomactsofkindness.org). Here you'll discover many ideas for school, home, and work along with lots of free resources.

So, dear reader, how's your day?

In Practice:

Consider some of the following as part of your daily activities. (This list is not exhaustive; feel free to add your own possibilities.)

- Pick up someone's trash.
- Extend a warm greeting to a stranger.
- Give up a parking space to someone.
- Plant a tree.
- Donate old clothes.
- Give to a worthy cause.
- Compliment a server at your favorite restaurant.
- Donate blood.
- Compliment a friend and post it on social media.
- Volunteer at the local animal shelter.
- Pay the toll for the driver behind you.
- Thank the janitor at your place of work.
- Always share a smile—lots of smiles.

For Journaling:

Compelling psychological research has demonstrated that being kind benefits not only others' but also our own well-being. Making kindness a regular part of our daily routine is a celebration of positivity, an appreciation of connection. Consider recording in your journal each day one random act of kindness. Watch what happens when you do.

Think About . . .

Rubber trees have seed pods that fling open and shoot the seeds for several yards in all directions. By the same token, we should distribute kindness freely. It will always find a place to germinate.

There Is No Emergency

Knowing trees,
I understand the meaning
of patience.
—HAL BORLAND

The following life strategy is not original to this book; it has shown up in numerous self-help presentations in one form or another. But this strategy is so important that it bears repeating. It will make a major difference in the quality of *your* life. Guaranteed.

Think about this statement: Life isn't an emergency!

Now this statement: We frequently take little events and *turn them into* major disasters or emergencies.

Both those statements are true, almost to the point of being facts of life. Nevertheless, we have a propensity to believe otherwise. We are given an assignment at work along with a deadline. Then what do we do? Our whole life revolves around that project. "If I don't get this done, I'll be sanctioned, demoted, or, even worse, fired. Got to get it done! Got to get it done!" Often to the exclusion of our family, our health, or our sanity, the project consumes our life and all our time. *IT'S AN EMERGENCY!*

No, it isn't.

I once had a student who was a confirmed neatnik. She couldn't leave for her classes unless her apartment was picture-perfect. All the towels had to be folded just right, her bed had to be made with absolutely no wrinkles, no dishes could be left in the sink, and no dust could appear on the living room table. *How can I go out into public knowing that my apartment is messy and disorganized? What will people think? I've got to clean it up! I've GOT to clean it up! IT'S AN EMERGENCY!*

No, it isn't.

We often turn routine activities into something they are not. We create artificial pressure on ourselves that becomes all-consuming and all-important. We manufacture an emergency that just isn't there. Blood pressure rises. The heart beats faster. The sweat glands activate. The temperature escalates. We self-induce our own pressure.

Pause in front of one or more oak trees, and you might sense that these majestic beings have an inner strength we sometimes ignore. (Oak trees are a widely used symbol of strength and endurance. As such, they are the national tree of several countries, including the United States.) Yet a forest of oaks is also one of escape—from the overpowering details of a schedule overflowing with Zoom meetings, self-induced assignments, and electronic commitments that, too often, overwhelm life. Oaks grow large and impressive, yet they are in no hurry to reach the sky. In their advancement, they stretch out their branches to take in the sunlight and embrace the wind. Their leaves offer an artistic pallet of colors in the fall and the spirit of rebirth in the spring. For the most part, oaks survive quite well in an environment that is both calm and deliberate. Their strength—their existence—takes place in a world unhurried and measured. Oaks show us that a well-lived life is one that eschews the invasiveness of self-induced emergencies.

When we can't meet deadlines or priorities, we often beat ourselves up. However, one of the most positive things we can do is admit that, in most cases, we create our own emergencies. That admission is a critical first step to becoming more peaceful. The reality is that things may not go as we want them to; that's part of the process. It's something we need to remember—and accept. Instead, step back, breathe deeply, move slowly, meditate. Make time, critical time, for you. Walk among trees, and absorb their presence. Pause, listen, feel. This is not wasted time; this is time you need to regroup and reconsider.

Is life an emergency?

No, it isn't.

In Practice:

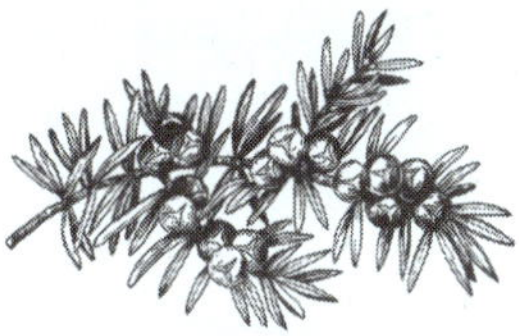

Here's a neat strategy: Every so often, give yourself a complaint-free day. As soon as you get out of bed, decide that this day will be completely free of any complaints or grievances. You will not complain, criticize, grumble, moan, or protest about anything during the entire day. (Not surprisingly, the more we find fault, the more the events of our lives turn into emergencies.) This cessation will be much harder than you might think, but it's something that will stick with you for a long time. You've changed an emergency into a reckoning—a realization that your attitude determines what is important and what is not.

For Journaling:

Consider making a list of some of the emergencies you've had in the past week, the past two weeks, or the last month. What events have unnecessarily taken up a lot of your time or caused you considerable anguish? Pick one of those events and describe its effects on you. How much time did you lose? What were some of your emotional reactions? Did you learn anything in the process? When we write about the supposed emergencies in our lives, we often discover that they are considerably less important than we originally thought.

Think About . . .

The boojum tree is known for its wild, twisting branches and jovial appearance. It's a "happy" tree, like its namesake character from a Lewis Carroll poem. Your recipe for a happy life: Include fun in your everyday activities. That's it. One ingredient, every day. Remember: a day without fun is like a boojum tree without branches.

Being Remembered

To be a tree and
read the memory of the leaves.
—DEJAN STOJANOVIC

Several years ago, I wrote a children's book titled *Around One Log: Chipmunks, Spiders, and Creepy Insiders.* It was about the variety of animal life throughout and around a fallen tree—now a weathered log deep in the forest. I invited young readers to notice the variety of animals in and around the tree: skipping bugs, some scooting lizards, several creepy-crawly spiders, and numerous critters slipping in and out of the slowly rotting wood. I informed readers that some creatures were only passing through while others had adopted the fallen tree as a new home.

My intent was to help youngsters become aware of the diversity of life in and around an ancient log. While the former tree may have been spectacular in its protracted life, that life takes on new meaning as it slowly decomposes on the forest floor. The formerly live tree may have harbored a succession of birds' nests, an enclave of slippery reptiles, or the buzz of selected insects. Yet even in death, it is a sanctuary for other life-forms as well as a home for occasional visitors.

In both life and death, it is a giving tree.

Everyone in the world is trying to live their lives as best they can. Many grow up, get an education, secure a job, get married, buy a home, pay a mortgage, have children, and slip into retirement. So, too, do we contend with crises, face hurdles, endure challenges, and make decisions that impact others. We also grow older. And eventually, like a tree in an old-growth forest, we die.

So here's life's ultimate question: When you die, how will you be remembered?

All the money you made? The expansive house you bought along with the expensive car parked in the equally expansive garage? The cruises you took or the villas you stayed in? Because you never missed a day of work and always attended every meeting on time? For all the toys you bought your kids or jewelry you gave your spouse? All your Facebook postings or Instagram photos?

Or when you die, will you be remembered for how you made a difference in the lives of others?

Like a tree.

In Practice:

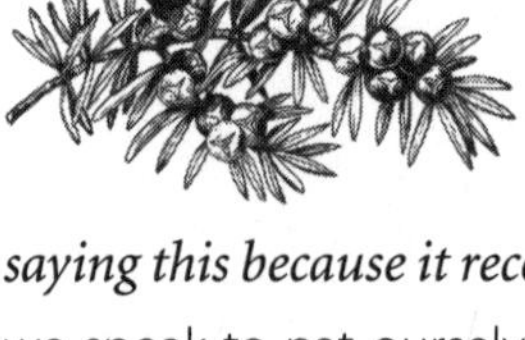

Whether you are chatting with someone or engaged in a protracted conversation with others, consider this: *Am I saying this for my own benefit, to promote my own ego? Or am I saying this because it recognizes or celebrates someone else?* All too often we speak to pat ourselves on the back rather than recognize another human being and their psychological needs. Or look at it this way:

Would you rather be remembered for how you celebrated you or how you celebrated someone else? Here are a few ideas for your consideration:

- "I understand what you're saying and would like to learn more."
- "You really cleared that up for me. Thanks for sharing."
- "I may disagree with you, but I appreciate your passion for this topic."
- "I'm wondering if there is another way we could look at this, an alternate view?
- "I wonder if you'd be interested in another point of view."

For Journaling:

Here's a challenging assignment for you. In your journal, make a list of ten items you'd like to be remembered for when you die. Or imagine someone you love was delivering your eulogy. What are the three most important things you would like them to share with the audience? Here's a list for your consideration. Which of these would you check?

- ☐ "She always gave her best to everyone she met."
- ☐ "He shared his laughter with everyone."
- ☐ "He was one of our community's hardest-working volunteers."
- ☐ "She never let anyone down. You could always count on her."
- ☐ "The moment you met him, you liked him. He was everybody's friend."
- ☐ "I'm certain his middle name was Kindness."
- ☐ "Our home was always filled with her cheer."
- ☐ "She had the most positive attitude of anyone I've ever met."

Think About . . .

Remember the tree where you built your first tree fort? Remember the backyard tree you always visited when you had something to get off your chest? Remember the tree that brought you colorful blossoms every spring? Trees are remembered for what they give, never for what they take away.

Life Is Not a Competition

In a forest of a hundred thousand trees,
no two leaves are alike.
And no two journeys along
the same path are alike.
—PAULO COELHO

The other day I came across a statement on one of my social media platforms. It made me pause and think a little deeper about where I am and where I can be:

> *I am in competition with no one. I have no desire*
> *to play the game of being better than anyone.*
> *I am simply trying to be better than*
> *the person I was yesterday.*

Like me, you've probably met people who want to outdo you; they want to prove how much better they are in a particular field or endeavor. They play a constant game of one-upmanship—citing all their accomplishments and honors, celebrities they've met, and accolades they've achieved in their lives. They are also the folks who hang a phalanx of certificates, diplomas, and awards on their office walls to impress anyone who enters. Their focus in life, it seems, is on advertising their accomplishments and trophies.

"I'm better than you" is often their message.

As a result, we often compare ourselves with these individuals, and unfortunately, that comparison is frequently negative. We feel inadequate, considerably less than perfect, and our self-concept suffers. Rather than being content with who we are and where we are going, we beat ourselves up because we don't measure up to another person's accomplishments. Instead of being grateful for what we have, we focus on what we don't have and prioritize our need to measure up to someone else's artificial standards.

Eastern redbuds demonstrate a better way.

Native to eastern North America, redbuds are small trees only growing to heights of twenty to thirty feet. They are distinguished by short trunks with wide spreading branches. But they are probably most famous for their brilliantly colored flowers, colorful foliage, and spectacular blooms.

Redbud flowers are a magical array of light pinks, dark magentas, and a robust sprinkling of whites. But the pinks draw the most attention. Small, blushing flowers adorn these trees in the spring. Clusters of these blooms grow up and down the lengths of the branches, making the tree seem like an enormous pom-pom befitting the Super Bowl or a World Cup soccer match. What makes them particularly unique is that all those flowers grow on bare branches.

Redbuds stand out as singular trees—one of a kind. They are exceptional because they are unlike any other tree. They do not copy the features of their contemporaries; their beauty is distinctive and unique. They do not compete with other trees; they flower on their own terms, in their own way.

The point, as embodied in the opening quote, is that when we begin comparing ourselves to others, we put our energy in the wrong place. We often become so focused on what someone else has that we lose sight of what *we* have. Consequently, our mental strength is sapped, and our direction is altered.

The solution is to catch ourselves whenever we compare ourselves to others. Our life should be lived on our terms; it should not be measured by others' accomplishments. Gently remind yourself every so often that you are on your own road. Being like someone else is not your goal; being better tomorrow than you are today should be. Don't compare yourself to others; it's emotionally exhausting, psychologically demanding, and detrimental to your growth and advancement.

Be like a redbud. Blossom on your own terms.

In Practice:

Social media exposes us to so many people who are successful, famous, wealthy, beautiful, or influential. As a result, we tend to compare ourselves to folks we don't know or have never met—and those comparisons are quite often toxic. They affect our psychological and emotional well-being. Instead, implement some of the following ideas, all of which can help you reduce how much you engage in comparisons:

- Recognize that comparing often has hurtful implications.
- Continuous comparisons lead to lower self-esteem.
- When we compare, we often match our lesser qualities with someone's better qualities.
- Know that you have positive qualities that the other person does not.

- Regularly celebrate the good in *your* life rather than the negatives.
- Spend more time admiring yourself—not those whom you've never met.

For Journaling:

How would you respond to the following: How much better are you today than you were yesterday? Write a short response and post it on your bathroom mirror, the top of your computer monitor, or as a Post-it note on your lunch box. Here are a few examples:

"I am better today than I was yesterday because I . . .

. . . spent time tossing a softball with my daughter."

. . . decided to take a painting class."

. . . helped a friend decorate her bedroom."

. . . told a stranger how much I liked her coat."

. . . took a stray cat to the animal shelter."

. . . shoveled my neighbor's sidewalk."

. . . donated some clothes to the Salvation Army."

. . . showed my niece how to ride a bicycle."

Think About . . .

Find a tall tree in your backyard, your neighborhood, or at a local park. Stand in front of it, and listen very carefully. Can you hear it? It's saying, "I am a valuable and unique individual, and I am worthy of others' respect. As a result, I stand tall." Now it's your turn to repeat.

Asking for Help

I found far more answers in the woods
than I ever did in the city.

—MARY DAVIS

Like you, I sometimes feel uncomfortable asking for help. Family, friends, and colleagues all lead busy lives. They have their own duties and obligations. Why should I add my need to their lives with my own request for assistance? It's a struggle I deal with many times.

A recent study out of Stanford University underscored our reluctance to ask for help. The researchers noted that most people are naturally inclined to help others, yet many of us struggle to reach out when we're in need. The authors suggested that we tend to underestimate others' willingness to provide help and overestimate how inconvenienced they would feel by the ask. Yet as the researchers also point out, giving and receiving help are natural parts both of humanity and a functional society.

When you ask someone for help, you acknowledge that that person has some degree of expertise or skill you may not. When a friend asks me to review something they have written, they are complimenting my talents as an author. By the same token, when I ask a colleague to show me how to upgrade the security of my computer, I am complimenting their technical skills.

Trees don't ask one another for help, but they give it nonetheless. Take, for example, a forest with several different species of trees. Scientific evidence has proven that trees of the same species will form communal relationships—cooperative groupings maintained through underground fungal networks. Not only do they share nutrients and water through these networks, but they also "communicate" with one another whenever a drought, disease, or insect attack is imminent. The trees can then alter their behavior to slow or halt any negative effects of those attacks.

Equally important, trees of different species also form underground alliances. This mutual admiration society fosters cooperative relationships that ensure the survival of all members. In short, the intelligence of the few benefits the endurance of many. In anthropomorphic terms, trees help one another survive by responding to calls for help. Everyone grows.

A substantial body of research shows that helping someone often promotes feelings of happiness, increases self-esteem and social connection, lowers stress levels and blood pressure, and even helps us live longer. Most interesting, however, is the undeniable truth that despite our misguided fears about asking for help, when we do, we are often seen as more engaged in social interactions.

Know that there is a natural hesitation to ask others for help. But you may discover that people are more willing to say yes than to decline the invitation. You may make a new friend or solidify a relationship. Above all, you'll see the importance of giving back to others.

The bottom line is that asking for help is not a weakness but a strength. It's a recognition that we all have different skill sets and that we can benefit one another by sharing our talents. Being a little fearful about asking for help is natural because we often think it makes us look incompetent, but the opposite is true. Humans crave human connections. Asking for and offering help are two of the best ways to establish and cement those relationships. It's a natural part of the social contract we have with one another.

Just like the underground connections of trees.

In Practice:

You can help normalize the helping process by providing assistance for others. Make an offer to feed the neighbor's cat while they're away for the weekend. Ask if you could read a book to a bedridden friend. Offer to pick up a neighbor's mail while they're on vacation. Mow an elderly person's yard or tidy up their garden. Drive someone to their doctor's appointment. Offer to coach a Little League team. Wash your next-door neighbor's car. By making these offers—giving help to others—you will become more comfortable requesting help for yourself.

For Journaling:

If you're somewhat uncomfortable about asking for help, start off by asking for small favors. For example, ask a neighbor to water your garden while you're on vacation. Ask a friend to help you select flowers for a sick colleague. Ask a relative to visit when you're feeling sick. Ask a colleague to help you with a computer issue. After each event, take a few minutes and write down your reactions to those requests. How did you feel as you were making the request? What kinds of emotions did you experience while that task was in progress? Take some time to focus on your internal reactions before, during, and after a request. Note any positive changes over time.

Think About . . .

You live your life to the fullest when you surround yourself with supportive friends. Perhaps that's why so many trees live in forests.

Your Definition of Success

Look at a tree. . . .
Let your awareness rest upon it.
How still they are, how deeply rooted in Being.
—ECKHART TOLLE

The greenery was all around. It spilled down from the mountains and flowed toward a rough and ragged shoreline. This was nature's palette—an artistic mélange of pigments characteristic of any Hawaiian journey. We were on the Road to Hana—a twisting, turning thoroughfare (a fifty-two-mile drive with 620 curves and fifty-nine bridges) that hugs the north shore of Maui and brings the vibrancy of this tropical paradise into sharp focus. With both hands firmly gripping the steering wheel, and Phyllis in charge of the photography, we stopped often to drink in the spreading landscape. One of our pauses was the Bamboo Forest.

We parked in front of the chain-link fence, grabbed our cameras, and walked back in time. Visions of *Jurassic Park* filled our eyes, and a soaring curtain of greenery overwhelmed us. Fully expecting a plodding diplodocus or two to wander past, we were taken by the rich array of bamboo plants ascending nearly forty feet into humid skies. Their height and abundance blocked the radiant sunlight so much a part of Hawaiian days.

Bamboo has its ancestral roots in the Eocene Epoch, evolving from prehistoric grasses approximately 30 to 40 million years ago. Although it has several treelike qualities (great heights, leafy canopies, flowers), bamboo is most certainly a member of the grass family. It originated in China, where over four hundred species grow today. Tall and hearty, humans have employed it over time for a range of uses including food, clothing, housing, transportation, toothbrushes, musical instruments, furniture, kitchenware, textiles, skincare products, flooring, weapons, and a writing medium. It is, evolutionarily speaking, one of the most successful of all plants.

How do you define your own success? Place a check mark in front of each of the following statements you sincerely believe to be true. Remember that this is a self-test, so be true to yourself.

- ☐ I have limitations, and I accept them.
- ☐ I am still a work in progress.
- ☐ I am grateful for the people in my life.
- ☐ I love, I am in love, and I am loved.
- ☐ I have made mistakes, but I have made peace with those mistakes.
- ☐ There is serenity in my life.
- ☐ I take care of my needs.
- ☐ I celebrate my achievements, large and small.

- ☐ I dream.
- ☐ I laugh at myself and with others.
- ☐ Life is a series of small steps, not necessarily big leaps.
- ☐ I embrace change; only through change does life improve.

How did you do? Did you place a check mark in front of all or most of these statements? Which ones made you unsure?

People often define success as something that is won. For example, a professional tennis player is successful if she wins Wimbledon or the US Open. A businessperson is successful if their company's stock improves exponentially. The person down the street is successful if her garden is selected as "Best in the Neighborhood." We often view success as a game or contest in which others determine the rules, conditions, and regulations. Our winning is determined by how others have shaped the competition.

True success is a do-it-yourself project!

Real success is personal; it's understanding yourself, your values, and your qualities as a human being. True success is not accumulating lots of points, money, or fame; it is being in touch with you. Most important, success is acknowledging the value of your personal qualities and being grateful for what you have to share with others. Real success is not completing an occasional contest that wins a gold medal, blue ribbon, or large chunk of money. The best kind of success is what we create for ourselves. Set your own goals, work toward them, and congratulate yourself when you meet them.

Right now, would you put a check mark in front of the following statement?

- ☐ My life is full of possibilities!

In Practice:

Sometimes we need little reminders of where we're going and how best to get there. What do experts say about success, and what is their advice about how to achieve it? You may want to collect several quotes or citations on success and post them in a place you see every day (vanity mirror, side of the refrigerator, coffee maker, back of the front door). Keep searching for new statements about success, and replace them every so often. Here are a few to get you started:

- "Success is the sum of small efforts—repeated day in and day out."—Robert Collier
- "Success is not the key to happiness. Happiness is the key to success. If you love what you are doing, you will be successful." —Albert Schweitzer
- "Success is peace of mind which is a direct result of self-satisfaction in knowing you did your best to become the best you are capable of becoming."—John Wooden
- "Success is getting what you want. Happiness is wanting what you get."—Dale Carnegie
- "Success isn't a result of spontaneous combustion. You must set yourself on fire."—Arnold H. Glasow
- "If you find it in your heart to care for somebody else, you will have succeeded."—Maya Angelou (one of my favorites)
- "Success consists of going from failure to failure without loss of enthusiasm."—Winston Churchill
- "Success is to be measured not so much by the position that one has reached in life as by the obstacles he has overcome." —Booker T. Washington

For Journaling:

Take some time daily to write down something successful you've done. Perhaps you cheered up a friend who's down, you picked up some trash alongside the road, you complimented a store clerk for good service, you helped your daughter learn how to kick a soccer ball, you finished writing the first chapter of your new book, you learned how to install an automobile battery, you signed up for that Italian cooking class, or you completed your first 10K race. Keep an ongoing record or chart. Refer back to it sometimes. Be sure to celebrate all your accomplishments.

Think About . . .

Sequoia trees stand tall and proud, as they have for thousands of years, a notice that self-respect is freedom from the expectations of others. It's a gift to ourselves.

Letter-Perfect Gratitude

If I am not thankful for the tree that stands
in front of me, I will never see the
forest that stands around me.
—CRAIG D. LOUNSBROUGH

As a college professor, I wanted students to know that they were much more than numbers or faceless participants in class. I wanted to build a community of learners in every course—a group that supported and celebrated one another as unique individuals with equally unique personalities. So, too, did I want them to know that their scholastic efforts were recognized and honestly celebrated.

In each class I made an effort to notice behaviors that went above and beyond the usual course requisites. Perhaps a student made a commanding argument about a controversial issue discussed in class. Maybe someone turned in an exceptional paper full of passion and intent. Or a student could have asked a penetrating question that steered a small group discussion into new territories.

Every so often, I would select one or two names, take some thank-you cards from my desk drawer, and write each of several students a personal note about how they contributed to the class, the learning community in that room, or their own education. I would hand-write this message of appreciation, put it into an envelope, and address the letter to their college address rather than their parents' or home address.

Here's a sample:

> Dear Megan:
> I wanted to take this opportunity to thank you for your comment on Tuesday about book banning during our discussion on the value of classroom libraries. Your view helped us understand an alternative viewpoint, particularly for young readers from marginalized communities. I look forward to more of your insights and thoughts in future sessions. Thank you so much for your contribution!
> Sincerely,
> Anthony D. Fredericks, EdD

Those thank-you messages were never mentioned in the course syllabus or in class. Neither did I ever contact students to see if they received their note or what they thought about it. Sometimes students would mention their appreciation in an e-mail or a subsequent class, but quite often there was no response—and I was fine with that. Those letters were not for my gratification; rather they were a commemoration of the work, time, and effort a student put into a course. The thank-you notes were recognitions of each individual, an acknowledgment of their contributions, and a celebration of individual good!

In their own way, trees also celebrate what is good and beautiful. Consider the spectacular rainbow eucalyptus (*Eucalyptus deglupta*) trees that grow in the rainforests of the Philippines, Indonesia, and Papua New Guinea. Standing nearly 250 feet tall, the rainbow eucalyptus is a colorful spectacle with its orange-tinted bark. Over time, that bark slowly peels away to reveal a spectacular array of greens, reds, oranges, grays, purples, and browns—a kaleidoscope of colors. Each time a tree sheds its bark, new and varied shades are revealed, so the trees are always producing a diversity of artistic patterns—each unique to a specific specimen. A forest of these trees is like an ever-evolving canvas of tints, hues, and colors—a rotating palette of pigments and blushes.

Rainbow eucalyptus trees give beauty to their environment, and they give back to their world. They celebrate an ecosystem by sharing a unique characteristic and a distinctive trait with natives and visitors alike. Theirs is a life full of giving—a life of celebration.

Walk into a nearby forest. If your senses are on full alert, the trees will send you a few thank-yous, too:

- The leaves of deciduous trees change into a rainbow of colors in the fall. "We're going to sleep soon but want to send you some bright colors to make your day a little better."
- During a spring day the wind will blow through the leaves. "Hey, I know you're resting under my branches, but I thought you might enjoy a gentle song, too."
- The thick, spreading branches of a broad tree in a city park create an area of shade. "I know it's hot out there, so I thought you might want to cool down under my branches. Stay as long as you want."

- Several trees have holes in which small mammals or birds build their homes and raise their young. "I like to care for others as much as possible. Perhaps you might want to join me and do the same."

People have the capacity and obligation to recognize the beauty of others. For example, take a few minutes each week and write a thank-you note (no e-mails; you want the sensation of putting pen to paper) to someone important in your life—a spouse, a parent, a child, a childhood friend, a close neighbor, a lover, a grandparent, a long-time colleague, a former college roommate, or a business associate. Select people from your past or present, each of whom would be deserving of a heartfelt note or friendly correspondence.

In your note, tell the recipient what you like most about them. Is it a sense of humor, an ability to tackle difficult challenges, a certain tenacity, or a willingness to help others? Whatever you admire in that person, write it down and provide one or two specific examples. Address the envelope, put a stamp on it, and drop it in the mail.

The single purpose of this activity is to demonstrate your gratitude for others in your life—previously and in the present. It is a simple act of sharing, a gift from the heart. Don't ask if a recipient has received the note or what they think about what you wrote. Let that come naturally. Never make it a condition of the act.

Imagine the feeling your note will have on the other person. They'll also be full of gratitude. Because you hand-wrote the note, they'll know you thought they were worthy enough for a personal contact instead of an all-too-common reliance on electronic communications. The recipient will feel your gratitude and may see fit to pay it forward to someone else in their sphere of influence. You will make their day.

Writing and mailing this note may seem a little time consuming, but it is worthwhile simply because it is seldom done. It celebrates and honors the qualities you admire most in others. You'll likely discover that you gain increased awareness of the positive qualities you enjoy in others in addition to those you discover about yourself.

Trees are always sending us acknowledgments and celebrations. Perhaps we should do the same.

In Practice:

Sit down, right now, and write someone a thank-you note. Not an e-mail or a text message—a hand-written message of support, encouragement, love, or validation. Think of someone among all the people in your life—family, friends, colleagues, associates, neighbors. Celebrate them, and let them know that you care. You don't need a reason to be nice. Other ways to share your recognition of others include a sincere smile, a loving hug, a shaking of hands, a warm pat on the back, a friendly comment, or even a simple, "I love you," will also do the trick, particularly when done every day.

For Journaling:

Every once in a while, take some time and write a thank-you note to yourself. What do you like about you? What do you appreciate about yourself? How are you growing and learning? Address the note to yourself, put a stamp on the envelope, and drop the letter in the mail. When the note arrives, savor it, enjoy it, and ponder it. Celebrate your life and who you are becoming.

Think About . . .

Many trees provide shelter, protection from sunlight and thunderstorms, and a welcoming home for various animals. If it's raining on someone else's parade, make sure you stop and give them some cover.

Facing Forces

I took a walk in the woods and
came out taller than the trees.
—HENRY DAVID THOREAU

Has someone ever offended you or said something unkind about you or your philosophy of life? Has anyone argued with you and told you that you "didn't know what you were talking about"? Has anyone insulted you or made you feel less than you are? Welcome to the club.

In our dealings with others, we often encounter folks who are unkind, unsupportive, or just plain mean. These folks think they know what's best for us or that their view of the world is more important than that of others. Their ego often gets in the way of good communication; they often insult without knowing the consequences of their actions. You and I and all the other people in this world are often targets of their verbal put-downs and resentment. And it hurts.

Interestingly, psychologists have noted a rise in that negative behavior over the past two decades. It seems that the busier people get, the more crowded their lives become, the more they tend to slight others in their orbit. Instead of embracing those around them, such people inadvertently push others away. Partly it's an act of self-preservation; partly it's to hold firm to their way of thinking—their way of surviving in a constantly evolving world. Intentional or not, what they do or say deeply affects us, and our happiness suffers accordingly. Our day is often determined by the behavior of others rather than by our own desires and dreams.

On a recent visit to New York, Phyllis and I, along with our best friends, journeyed to the National September 11 Memorial and Museum. Just outside the museum is a Callery pear tree, known as the "Survivor Tree." The tree had been pulled from the rubble of the 9/11 attack with a charred trunk, shattered branches, and snapped roots. It looked dead but was tenaciously clinging to life. It was removed from the rubble and placed in the care of the New York City Department of Parks and Recreation. After lots of dedicated care it eventually recovered. Today, vibrant limbs arc from the gnarled stumps, healthy leaves spring forth from its branches, and it reaches toward the sky with vigor and determination. Cards, letters, posters, and occasional balloons festoon its surrounding enclosure—mementos from tourists and residents in homage to its tenacity, resiliency, and revival.

It is an icon of survival.

As was that tree, we are also assaulted by the negative behaviors of others. Quite often, we hold on to these injustices, allowing them to fester and grow inside us. We often believe that we are less than we are; what others do to us takes precedence over what we believe to be true internally. Their actions often override our quest for happiness.

It doesn't have to be that way. Instead of allowing these injustices to consume us, we need to let go. In the grand scheme of things, they are minor troubles rather than major impediments. They are the kinds of small stuff that fester and grow into big stuff, sapping our growth and limiting our joy. Yet by letting these behaviors pass by us rather than consuming us, we assure ourselves of an inner peace—a relaxation of mind and soul. In turn, you'll find yourself less defensive and calmer.

Let it go. Keep growing outward and upward—like that Callery pear in New York City.

In Practice:

People who put us down are often trying to exert some form of control, get attention, or express their own negativity. Dealing with those individuals is frequently challenging, but there are ways to respond:

- Don't retaliate, because it just eggs them on. Instead, come back with something kind, which often throws them off their game.
- If the insults come from someone you know, be sure to tell them how you feel. What are your emotions? ("I really get upset when you talk to me that way.")
- Often, those who insult others are just looking for some kind of reaction, and the reaction just fuels their intent. Instead, ignore them. If necessary, turn your back and walk away.
- Hold on to your self-concept. Remember that you are an important person. What you think about yourself is far more significant than how others may see you.

For Journaling:

One of the best ways of dealing with people who put you down is to remind yourself of all your positive qualities and characteristics. Take the time to record a list of some of your outstanding features or personality dynamics. For example,

- I reach out to other people when they ask for help.
- I always bring a smile to work.
- When I start something, I always finish it.
- I'm a little bit better today than I was yesterday.
- I'm a good person.
- I always offer a helping hand to others.
- Know what? I love me.

You may also want to craft a list of some of the good things others say about you. Refer to it often.

Think About . . .

It was a magnificent southern live oak standing royally against a resplendent Louisiana skyline. It had survived hurricanes and drought, insects and floods. A branch here and there was cracked, and a few leaves were missing, but it had endured and was admired by humans for two centuries—not just for its beauty, but also for how it had survived the hardships of nature.

For the Love of Peaches

If you want to be happy for a year, plant a garden;
if you want to be happy for life, plant a tree.
—ENGLISH PROVERB

The two sprouts arrived in late April—prime planting time for Redhaven peach trees in Hardiness Zone 6B. I dug deep holes in the dark earth and ensured that the two self-pollinating trees were subject to full sunlight. I deposited several shovelfuls of loamy dirt into each hole. A light application of fertilizer and a soaking from an adjacent spigot completed the process.

It was a brutal summer. Rain was sporadic and scarce. Temperatures rose consistently into the nineties, and dry winds frequently scoured the Middle Atlantic region. Throughout June, July, and August I stood beside my adopted trees with water hose in hand and great anticipation in mind. Visions of "blue-ribbon, all-purpose peaches with almost fuzzless skin over firm, creamy textured yellow flesh" danced through my head.

Autumn winds blew in, and temperatures began to plummet. I refertilized and carefully tended my charges. Temperatures continued to drop, and winter arrived with a chilly vengeance. In late December a brutal snowstorm dropped from the skies. Every hour I peered into the yard to monitor events. The following morning, I rushed to the window. The trees were nowhere to be seen. A smothering blanket of whiteness had concealed everything under eighteen inches in height. I strapped on my boots, grabbed a shovel, and went out to rescue them.

Over the months, I gave my saplings lots of TLC. Theirs was a protected environment—one maintained and mastered by a focused individual bent on their ecological success. I was their guardian and their monitor. They would succeed in spite of environmental threats—of that, I would be sure.

Peach trees are just trying to be peach trees. They'll never change into apple trees, pear trees, or persimmons. Far be it for me to suggest, or even try, to alter their genetic destiny. They are who they are.

So it is with friendships. A friend is not a friend if all we want to do is change that person into something more like ourselves. Friendships thrive because of a respect for differences, an embrace of alternative philosophies. If we say, "I'll let you be my friend, but you have to think just like I think or act like I act, or it's no deal," then that relationship is doomed to die. Trying to change people into something they are not does not justify a friendship, nor does it ensure its existence.

Now, practice that alliance with others. Don't try to change them; instead, accept their needs and protect them in their journey. Love them the way they are, just like you would with trees—two peach trees.

In Practice:

Find your own tree—one just starting its life as a small sapling or one that has been around for several years. Adopt it, make it your own, take it under your wing, care for it as though it were your child or aging parent. Give it your unconditional love. Talk to it, wrap your arms around it, lie under its branches, take a picnic in its shade, take photos in various seasons, and be one with your charge. Notice how you feel in its presence; notice your lack of judgment or criticism. Despite its shape, the feel of its bark, the arc of its branches, or the critters in its canopy, this tree is now your companion, your constant comrade.

Notice, too, the peace you enjoy in its company, the calming of your mind, the strength of your soul, your measured breath and unhurried thoughts. It is your pal, your buddy, your confidant. You have accepted it, and in return it gives you strength and comfort. No need to change it, for it will always be what it is: your friend.

For Journaling:

Good friendships are always based on positivity and optimism. You can promote that in several ways: celebrating friends' achievements, suggesting common activities, talking about the good things in a friend's life, keeping complaints about things in your life to a minimum, celebrating humorous events, and—of course—smiling . . . a lot!

Make a list of three people you love unconditionally. Then, in your journal, write what you do to maintain that love for each of those individuals. What do you share? What do you discuss with each one? How are you able to accept each individual as an important part of your life? Which of those individuals reminds you most of a tree?

Think About . . .

In your life, do someone a favor and don't ask for or expect anything in return. Magnolia trees always give you large fragrant flowers. They never expect reciprocity.

Temporary Shadows

Trees give peace
to the souls of men.
—NORA WAIN

It stood alone—a solitary red maple alongside the perimeter of Conneaut Lake in northwestern Pennsylvania (forty-six miles south of Erie, Pennsylvania). It was still early spring, and its branches were devoid of any nascent buds—the harbingers of a healthy life. Those appendages reached out in myriad directions—like a woody octopus flailing in shallow waters. Its silhouette was highlighted against a graying sky; a foreboding bank of rain clouds was arcing in from the northwest. There were sunlit breaks here and there, and the tree captured the evolving sky with both grace and solemnity.

The tree's bark was a panache of muted browns and splotches of coffee-colored hues. Scattered across its magnificent limbs was a random assembly of burls clinging tenaciously to aged branches. It was evident that this red maple had taken on much in its life and had continued to stand proud against the forces that would weaken it or cause it to topple into the placid waters of the lake.

It had endured much and survived—quite well.

We were there to observe the total eclipse of the sun on April 8, 2024. It was a new venture—one that had been on our to-do list for several months. Arriving earlier in the afternoon we had secured a picnic table and a favorable sight line to the sky. Along with about two hundred other skywatchers, we waited patiently for the rain clouds to part, the sky to open, and the sun and moon to perform their celestial dance in front of a most admiring crowd. It was to be a two-minute-and-thirty-one-second solar eclipse—an event filled with amazement, delight, and the euphoria of an enraptured crowd replete with eclipse-proof sunglasses.

At 3:14 PM, with the moon covering a significant portion of the sun, a darkness began to settle over the land. In short order, the crowd began a countdown from ten to one. Instantly, everyone erupted in cheers and howls; excitement was rampant. The joy was contagious. Celestial history had been made.

Nearby streetlights flickered on, a flock of paddling ducks headed for the protection of cattails, and dogs looked nervously upward as a long, dark shadow covered the land. All the semblance of night surrounded us as though a master switch had been moved to OFF. We knew the blackness was temporary, but it was a celestial phenomenon that wouldn't reappear in the United States until August 23, 2044.

For all of that two-and-a-half minutes the crowd continued to cheer. Adjectives flew and exclamations were shared with passion and admiration. I watched the tree, now enveloped in that powerful shadow, standing patiently by the edge of the lake. It stood, as it had for decades, as a totem for the surrounding environment—a persistent beacon of life and strength.

The great shadow covered it, but that darkness was temporary. The tree would continue its existence as the magnificent tree it had always been. The obscurity did not alter it in any way—neither during the event, nor for any time afterward. The red maple continued to maintain its tree-ness as it always had, as it always would.

I reminisced. Too often we let small events or infrequent shadows become a source of major darkness. We see a personal slight as a significant catastrophe, a colleague's frown as a momentous disaster, a harsh word as an earth-shattering and forever attack on our personality. An expression, gesture, or sideways glance can turn our day into one of self-loathing or constant frustration. In turn, we internalize the negatives and ignore the positives of our being.

For me, the solution is in the words of that classic Beatles song (1970): "Whisper words of wisdom. Let it be!"

Recognize that the anger, bad attitude, or wrath of others is not part of who you are. That's their business; that's their burden, not yours. Refuse to accept their intent to change your day or alter your attitude. Their shadow may temporarily sweep over your face, but it won't change you. Their discontent is their problem, not yours.

Yes, some people want their shadows to affect us in detrimental ways. Don't accept it. In so doing, you'll appreciate the sunshine on the other side. Your mental outlook will be robust. Your self-concept will continue to be positive.

Or to requote four famous philosophers: "Let it be!"

In Practice:

Lots of people try to rise up by putting others down. There's some sort of satisfaction in thinking that they are better than others, more important than their fellow citizens. They try to enhance their egos by tearing down those of others. When we absorb those negative statements, we allow them to control our day and our feelings. Take some time, every day if necessary, to tell yourself that they have the right to determine their own day—and that you, and you alone, have the right to control how your day will evolve. Absorbing the bad attitudes of others diminishes our self-worth and self-satisfaction. As soon as you get up in the morning, choose your day. Then stick to it.

For Journaling:

Try beginning your day with a positive journal entry—one that clearly establishes the kind of day you would like to enjoy. Do this as soon as you rise; make it your goal. Here are a few examples:

- This will be a great day because I know some good things are going to happen.
- Today, I'd like to share my happiness with the world—one person at a time.
- I promise to make the lives of all my colleagues just a little bit better today.
- I can't wait to share some sunshine with those I meet today.
- Watch out, day. Here I come.

Think About . . .

On a recent walk, I found myself observing a solitary chestnut oak. I carefully watched this tree—leaves gently rustling in the wind, branches reaching for the sun, some squirrels playing around its base, and a solemnity that was both calming and reflective. It reminded me that too many people are so anxious about living in the negative that they often forget to live in the positive.

Part IV

Root for Yourself (and Others)

Gaining Inner Peace

Every leaf speaks bliss to me,
fluttering from the autumn tree.
—EMILY BRONTË

Meeting at 9:00 AM. Interview at 9:45 AM. Project due at noon. Client at 1:30 PM. Another meeting at 2:30 PM. Rush hour traffic at 5:00 PM. Soccer practice for Jimmy. Piano lessons for Susie. Fix clogged toilet. Make dinner. Feed cat. Pay bills. Check e-mails. Social media news. Etc. Etc. Etc.

Busy, busy, busy! It seems as though our lives and our schedules are packed with an abundance of to-dos and an avalanche of gotta-get-these-dones. We are rushed and frequently out of time. Our minds are clogged with self-induced emergencies and complications. Life has become one giant crisis after another. We often have the mistaken belief that every minute must be filled with something important. The day is short, so we only have so much time to get in everything.

Rush. Rush! *Rush!*

Time to *s-l-o-o-o-o-w d-o-w-w-w-w-n.* All this running around and trying to get everything checked off our to-do list takes up a lot of energy and generates too much frantic thinking. We are driven by an overcrowded schedule that sucks the motivation from our lives. Life is no longer enjoyable; it is endured. By the end of the day, we are exhausted, drained, and depleted. Then we have to do it all over again tomorrow.

Rush. Rush! *Rush!*

Consider the eastern hemlock tree, often cited as one of the slowest-growing trees in the world. With an average annual growth rate of between twelve and twenty-four inches, it takes its time ascending to its full height—up to 175 feet tall. It's in no hurry. The eastern hemlock seems to have embraced an ecological reality that slowing down can have a direct impact on one's longevity. As proof, arborists have noted that these trees can live on average for roughly 800 years, with one ancient specimen surviving for 988 years. Eastern hemlocks are about ten times slower in their growth than most other trees throughout North America.

The lesson is clear. A hurried lifestyle is not advantageous to our mental well-being or our psychological growth. Trying to get everything done doesn't simplify our life; it adds frenzy and stress. It creates a nonstop succession of emergencies, each more critical than the last.

Instead, listen to the eastern hemlock:

> Go slow; grow large.
>
> Go slow; grow old.

In Practice:

When we take the time to meditate, practice mindfulness, relax, contemplate, daydream, or just take a nap, we are giving ourselves permission to slow our lives. We are putting a premium on the value of inner peace rather than on satisfying an endless string of external obligations. We become less distracted by what we want and more focused on what we need. The slowed life, the peaceful life, enhances our concentration, improves our outlook, and adds to our longevity. So, too, does it give us extended opportunities to enjoy ourselves and share love with others. Slow down; watch what happens. You may be surprised.

For Journaling:

One of the most important things you can do daily is to reserve time for yourself. Carve out at least ten to fifteen minutes every day (for example, just after you get up, during a lunch break, immediately after dinner, or just before bedtime)—time for you to step back and just be, to regroup and reconsider, to put a pause in your activities and focus on you. Take this time to record your thoughts, itemize your feelings, or write about some of your emotions. What's going on in your head?

Or use your journal to doodle, draw, invent, create, imagine, outline, fabricate, concoct, or dream. Nothing fancy, nothing elaborate. Remember, this is your time—do with it what you want. There's no assignment, no grades. This is something you need. Every. Single. Day.

Think About . . .

Anyone who has walked a long trail through an old-growth forest will understand the following: taking time to *be* is a major element in a fulfilling life, a necessary component of self-satisfaction.

Be a Model of Positivity

Trees are poems the earth
writes upon the sky.
—KAHLIL GIBRAN

Psychologists note that negative comments frequently increase our anxiety level. Research has also convincingly demonstrated that a stream of negative comments damages key structures that regulate our memory, feelings, and emotions. These, in turn, may cause long-term reactions that can negatively affect our sleep, appetite, sex life, and daily functioning.

Sadly, there has been a noticeable increase in workplace negativity over the past several years. One explanation for this increase is that we have legitimized criticism via the Internet. For example, think about any product you have purchased on Amazon. Everything from books to moccasins to chain saws is subject to a review. We can give a product a rating of one to five stars *and* include comments about its performance or lack thereof. We can tell others exactly how we feel about a product, whether it's worth the money we spend for it, and whether others should even purchase that product. What's more, we can do it anonymously without fear of retribution or rebuke.

Criticism is inescapable. At some point, someone is going to criticize something you've said, how you drive in rush-hour traffic, the style of shirts you wear, how you tend your garden, or the paintings in your living room.

It's inevitable.

Forester Peter Wohlleben, in his celebrated book *The Hidden Life of Trees* (2016), makes a case for trees' sociability. He states, "As a forester, I learned that trees are competitors that struggle against each other, for light, for space. . . . Trees are very interested in keeping every member of this community alive." At times, that may mean restricting the growth of branches to allow more light into a given area of the forest; at other times it may mean an underground communication system that allows individual members of a forest community to interact with one another.

Although it's an anthropomorphic perspective, Wohlleben makes a case for the value of trees "playing nice" with one another. That is to say, trees, just like humans, prosper best within a supportive environment. When each individual reaches out and supports other individuals within a community, everyone prospers. Everyone grows.

Criticism depresses that advancement.

Criticism doesn't build relationships, and it certainly doesn't make our world or our local community a better place. People known for their criticism are not people we want to be around. They don't build us up; rather, they are intent on tearing us down—negative comment by negative comment. That's never a good thing.

A countermeasure is to serve as a model of positivity: someone who not only embraces the concept of human-to-human kindness but shares it in almost every encounter throughout the day. This may include a pleasant comment to the plumber fixing your dishwasher, a cheerful remark to the new neighbor who moved in just down the block, a wave and a greeting to the lifeguard at the community pool, a brief conversation with the checkout lady at the lumber store, a sincere thank-you to someone who offered some needed advice, or a gracious "Good morning" to the flight attendant when you're on a journey to visit grandkids.

Know that your positive outreach won't eliminate rampant criticism, but perhaps it will help make someone else's day a little brighter, a little more tolerable. When that happens, others may want to pass along that positivity.

Bottom line: Envision yourself as a model of positivity. No fame, no fortune, but it's certain you will discover something quite amazing. The positivity you share with others will come back to you many times over.

In Practice:

Thinking optimistically doesn't mean you ignore or circumvent some of life's unpleasantness. Adopting a positive attitude simply means you approach challenges with a more productive mindset. You anticipate the best, not the worst. Here are two strategies for your consideration:

- **Be aware of your thoughts.** Do you tend to think more negatively or more positively as you go through your day? If you find yourself with more negative thoughts, pause and think how you could turn those around.
- **Talk regularly with yourself in more positive ways.** For example, *This project is really wearing me down, but if I can just stick with it a little longer, I think I can make it work.* There is convincing research

that this simple activity can constructively affect how you deal with stress, in addition to reorienting your emotions.

For Journaling:

According to researchers at the Mayo Clinic, " personality traits such as optimism and pessimism can affect many areas of our health and well-being. The positive thinking that usually comes with optimism is a key part of effective stress management. "To help you move in a more positive direction, one often cited recommendation is to maintain a special gratitude journal. A sincere focus on gratitude changes your perspective and reorients your focus. Not only does it change your outlook, gratitude also reinforces it when you make that change a daily practice.

Each day write one or two sentences about things for which you are grateful. Here are two examples: "I am grateful for my children, who bring me so much joy and happiness every day." "I am grateful for my friend Jack, who always has a kind word for everybody." Notice how those grateful statements, when crafted regularly, have the power to alter your thinking in a more positive direction.

Think About . . .

That tree there has a scarred exterior. That tree over there has several broken branches. See that tree? It's missing a lot of leaves. Rule of the forest: You'll see what you want to see. If you want to see negative, that's what you'll find. But if you want to see positive . . .

Learning to Forgive . . . Ourselves

Deep down, at the molecular heart of life,
the trees and we are essentially identical.
—CARL SAGAN

We often beat ourselves up for a personal mistake, a professional slight, an error in judgment, or a social accident. We hang on to our guilt and constantly blame ourselves for weeks or months afterward. We capture and tenaciously hold on to an emotional burden filling our lives with anger and resentment.

We are in a funk—about ourselves.

As humans, we make mistakes. We say or do things we don't mean to. We may lose our temper with a child for no reason at all. We may tell one of our colleagues something about their work that has no basis in fact. Perhaps we tear into a clerk because they gave us the wrong change after a transaction. We may forget an important holiday or even an anniversary. Afterward, we realize that our behavior was inappropriate, unnecessary, and, at times, hurtful. As a result, we experience guilt, often descending into a period of self-blame that tugs at our emotional strings.

It's time for some liberation.

Being able to forgive ourselves is a critical part of our emotional stability and personal growth. By doing so, we give ourselves permission to learn from our mistakes and make necessary changes in our lives. In short, we take ownership of our behavior—a possession that results in greater compassion and self-love. Self-forgiveness is also an acknowledgment that we are imperfect creatures who deserve a measure of personal acceptance and the opportunity to change.

All too often, we hold on to internal guilt for long periods of time. Yet in forgiving ourselves, we have an opportunity to break that cycle and move into new arenas of positive change. Forgiving ourselves is a way of parting with the past and moving toward the future. There's another side effect of self-forgiveness, too. Letting go of past guilts gives us more opportunity to open up with others, foster more meaningful relationships, and create deeper channels of understanding.

If there was ever a tree that needed a measure of self-forgiveness, the castor bean tree would be an ideal candidate. It is a frequent addition to many ornamental gardens. Often ascending to heights of about forty feet, it is a fast-growing plant that often looks more like a shrub than a tree. Although it originated in Africa, it can now be found in many parts of the southern and eastern United States.

In ancient times, the oil in castor tree seeds was used as a fuel for lamps. In more modern times it has been used in paints and varnishes, for water-resistant coatings, in high-performance motor oils, as well as in soaps, inks, and plastics. But it is known most as a medicine. Readers of a certain age may remember getting a spoonful of castor oil as a child in order to treat constipation. (One advertisement for Fletcher's Castoria proclaimed that "It's safe and gentle—as a child's laxative should be—and it works thoroughly and effectively.")

But, there's a hidden side to castor tree beans. They also contain ricin, one of the world's deadliest natural poisons. It has been estimated that this toxin is six thousand times more poisonous than cyanide and twelve thousand times more poisonous than rattlesnake venom. The oil from as few as four seeds can kill an average-sized adult. Suffice it to say, ricin is removed from castor oil during processing.

Here's something to think about. Forgiving ourselves for past behaviors involves

- Taking an honest look at who we are
- Recognizing that each of us has certain shortcomings, and that
- We all have the capacity and ability to grow and improve our lives

As psychologists tell us, self-forgiveness means taking ownership of our behaviors as well as of their consequences. Blaming others is counterproductive to positive change. Telling ourselves that *It wasn't my fault* dismisses the proprietorship we need to move forward in our lives. Trying to convince ourselves that it will never happen again is a blockade to reflection and positive growth. Ultimately, forgiving ourselves means a sincere recognition that perfect humans don't exist, but better humans are a real possibility.

In extension, we may wish to offer some forgiveness to ricin. That's because it has also been scientifically cited as a potential anticancer (lymphoma) agent.

In Practice:

As appropriate, engage in regular meditation. Take ten to fifteen minutes each day to consider who you are and how you can change. Focus on how you can be less judgmental about yourself as well as how you might become more kind to yourself. Many books offer meditation instruction on how you can make peace with yourself. Here are three recommendations:

- *The Miracle of Mindfulness: The Classic Guide to Meditation by the World's Most Revered Master* by Thich Nhat Hanh (2021)
- *How to Meditate: A Guide to Self-Discovery* by Lawrence LeShan (2020)
- *Practical Meditation for Beginners: 10 Days to a Happier, Calmer You* by Benjamin W. Decker (2018)

For Journaling:

One of the ways often suggested to get the process of self-forgiveness started is to write a forgiveness letter to yourself. Provide the specific details of the action you committed—or forgot—and write a sincere apology to yourself. You may wish to keep this letter in a secure location and glance at it every so often as a reminder that you are moving in a positive direction.

Think About . . .

It was a splendid sycamore standing along the edge of the park. Its branches reached skyward; its roots held fast to the soil. Its crown was lush and green; its years were in the hundreds. These are all good reminders that the best kind of success is that which we create for ourselves.

Regaining You

A tree's wood is also its memoir.

—HOPE JAHREN

In Spanish, it's known as *asesina de árboles* (tree killer). To botanists, it is the strangler fig (*Ficus aurea*)—a murderous species that takes advantage of a host tree, systematically killing it over time.

This tree strangles life.

Endemic to Florida, the Caribbean, and Central America, these trees begin their life as a sticky seed high up on a tree branch—a seed typically deposited by the wind or a wandering animal. There it germinates and thrives as an epiphyte in the humid tropical atmosphere. As it grows, it sends long roots down the trunk of the host tree. Over time, the roots wrap their way around the host's trunk, expand, and eventually form a unique latticework that encircles the host's trunk many times.

Eventually the host tree is completely entwined. The stranger fig's roots are totally constricting the trunk, surrounding the host's roots, and cutting off nutrients and water. In addition, the fig develops a thick canopy that blocks sunlight from reaching the host. The host eventually dies and is subjected to the forces of decomposition, leaving a vibrant fig with a hollow trunk where the host used to be.

A tree that slowly strangles. A tree that robs others of their lives.

A friend early in her life also experienced a type of strangulation —one that squeezed her soul and choked her being for long years. Unbeknownst, she married a controlling and manipulative individual. For years, she was mentally abused by someone who professed to love her. He called her stupid. He ridiculed her, he was rude to her, he blamed her for anything that went wrong, and he would sometimes go for days without speaking to her or acknowledging her presence.

She began an affair; she contemplated suicide. Her life was spinning out of control; she was desperate and depressed. Then, on a whim, she began to write, poetry mostly. There was solace in her words, comfort in their meaning. It was escape from a downward spiral, a cautious reentry into a world of security and veneration.

Her body was down to skin and bones. She suffered a nervous breakdown. She was losing her ability to think, to work, or to handle life. Words were her sole comfort—poetic words of escape, change, and rebirth. They were her bulwark against daily terrors. Slowly, ever so slowly, she discovered that poetry gave her a voice—and resurrection. Then, one night, she found unusual strength in those words. She finally told her husband she was tired of being called names, tired of all the disrespect, tired of him blaming her for everything that went wrong, and tired of a lifeless life. And so, on a cold Friday night in January, she ended fourteen years of mental strangulation by leaving and never looking back.

Many people endure their own personal suffocations. Their self-respect suffers due to the inhumanity of others—others who gag our feelings and stifle our emotions. Like a strangler fig, those individuals squeeze our being and asphyxiate our existence. In turn, we are left as a shell of our former selves . . . for long years.

Escaping that murderous behavior takes an enormous amount of emotional energy. You often feel powerless over your own life because someone else owns it; someone controls you. Their actions and behaviors determine your actions and behaviors—a vicious and frequently unending cycle.

As appropriate, seek counseling services. Know that professionals are available in your local community who will listen to your story and offer strategies and assistance. These include mental health organizations, counseling referral services, psychological assistance agencies, crisis lifelines, national helplines, and mental health treatment referral centers. Also invite friends and colleagues to stand by you to provide guidance and direction. Embrace the company of others in your journey of renewal.

> I am not who I was a year ago, and
> that brings me so much peace.
> —Unknown

In Practice:

You can begin to regain your personal power one small step at a time. Craft a daily affirmation ("I am a good person full of life and laughter") and write it down. Pen a personal compliment for yourself ("My inner strength is standing up for myself, advocating for what I believe"). Write yourself a thank-you note ("Thank you [name] for your loving nature and giving attitude"). Know that when you do, you are taking back your life slowly and ever surely. You are back in charge of what you believe, who you are, and who you want to be. Most important, you begin to see improvement—and possibilities.

For Journaling:

If you're in a toxic relationship, practice some positive self-talk—every day. Record a conversation with yourself about where you are and where you should be. Focus on your strengths, your assets, your "goodness." Use your journal to outline how you are bolstering your self-respect, giving you strength and courage to advocate for yourself. Write about the advantages of building healthy relationships, renewing old friendships, spending more time with family, and enlarging your social circle. Then become an active member of your community: volunteer, take a class, pursue a new hobby, join with people who share your goals. Surround yourself with like-minded individuals. Reach out. Constantly.

Think About . . .

Ever stood in the middle of a magnificent redwood forest on a foggy summer morning? If so, then you'll understand this quote from Judy Garland: "Always be a first-rate version of you, instead of a second-rate version of somebody else."

Advice from a Tree

A tree has roots in the soil, yet reaches to the sky.

—WANGARI MAATHAI

Go into any Internet search engine and type in "Advice from a tree" or "The wisdom of trees," and you will most likely discover the following item. It's been around for a while, and it occasionally pops up on posters, T-shirts, and all sorts of knickknacks in gift shops at botanical gardens and national parks.

Advice from a Tree

Stand tall and proud.
Sink your roots into the earth.
Be content with your natural beauty.
Go out on a limb.
Drink plenty of water.
Remember your roots.
Enjoy the view.

Good advice! But take a moment and look at the second and sixth statements in the advice. Roots. They're both about roots. Must be something important. Yes it is.

What you might see is a commitment to staying grounded, a belief in who you are and what you stand for. It is an affirmation of your inner being—what you think, believe, and support, what makes you who you are and also who you can become.

Several years ago, I opened a section of a Selected Topics in Education course by asking my undergraduate students the following: "Do you believe in yourself?" There was instant quiet. I waited, then asked the question a different way: "Jeremy, in what ways do you believe in yourself?" "Abby, in what ways do you believe in yourself?" "Jamie, in what ways do you believe in yourself?" After long pauses, students began to proffer some responses. Not unexpectantly, most of their contributions revolved around religious matters, political stances, and axioms from a required philosophy course.

The lesson's focus was on the importance of self-concept—a critical aspect in how students of any age learn. It is also an aspect of the educational process that doesn't get a lot of attention. But it makes a difference, not only in every educational encounter, but also in how individuals see themselves and their place in the world. By definition, self-concept is a personal knowledge of who we are, a collection of intrinsic beliefs about ourselves. As you might expect, a positive self-concept is critical to every learning experience as much as it is necessary for a satisfactory life.

But it's also important in another way. Roots.

A visit to Sequoia National Park would be incomplete without time spent with one of its most iconic trees—the General Sherman. This tree is gigantic, nearly incomprehensibly so. The estimated weight of the trunk is 1,385 tons, its overall height is 274.9 feet, its circumference is 102.6 feet at ground level, its maximum diameter is 36.5 feet, and its average crown spread is 106.5 feet. The overall volume of its trunk measures 52,500 cubic feet, thus making it the largest-known living, single-stem tree on Earth.

But what may be particularly noteworthy is the fact that this tree's roots spread out over more than an acre—an embrace of over 90,000 cubic feet of soil. That mass of matted roots has to maintain the equilibrium of a tree that weighs nearly three million pounds (the standing weight of 120 school buses or the takeoff weight of more than three Boeing 747-400 airplanes). It is certain that this tree's longevity (ca. 2,200 years), as well as its commanding beauty, is ultimately due to the strength of its roots. That strength is admired by throngs of human visitors who stand in appreciation of its towering presence and commanding stature.

Strong roots, strong life.

Self-concept—a belief in, and a connection to, our inner being—is what keeps us grounded, what keeps us rooted. That grounding helps us withstand forces that can topple us, just like the General Sherman's roots help it withstand fierce storms and powerful winds.

Insecurity is when we beat ourselves up for minor mistakes or insignificant infractions. It often comes from a lack of self-concept. We embrace negative thoughts and turn those thoughts into major events and major obstacles. Sometimes we're consumed by what we cannot do rather than by what is possible. All too often, we see our lives as imperfect. Rootless.

Our inner reality is our bulwark against the world. It is our strength and our ultimate determination. Believing in ourselves gives us the same strength as a tall tree deeply rooted in the earth. Or as Ralph Waldo Emerson once said, "What lies behind us and what lies before us are tiny matters compared to what lies within us."

In Practice:

You can strengthen your self-concept by incorporating the following suggestions into your daily life. Each one has a positive influence on your personal image, on the roots of who you are:

- Acknowledge your worth. You are an important person.
- Challenge your negative thoughts and beliefs.
- Each day, give yourself at least one positive affirmation.
- Avoid unflattering comparisons with others.
- Make a list of things you admire about yourself.
- Set boundaries in your relationships.
- Divest yourself of negative people.
- Embrace the wisdom of trees.

For Journaling:

One of the biggest barriers to a positive self-concept is self-doubt: that little voice in the back of our heads that questions our abilities and holds us back from some of our life goals or our true potential. We can effectively deal with those self-doubts by adapting a growth mindset—a constant belief that we can improve and grow over time (rather than convincing ourselves that we must remain mired in the same place). When we remind ourselves of our strengths and accomplishments, we help ourselves realign our lives with positive affirmations. Here's a daily question to help you see the best in yourself: *What do I believe about myself?* Frame the answer using positive words—*I believe that I share love with every member of my family*—and record those responses.

Alternatively, make it a regular practice, perhaps weekly, to record what you like about you—not what your sister thinks, nor your neighbor down the street, nor the counterperson at your local McDonald's. What do you like about you right here, right now? No negative thoughts allowed!

Think About . . .

As mentioned earlier, redbud trees are some of the most beautiful trees of spring. Their first several months of growth are devoted to developing strong roots, so they are not very large for the first two or three years. Remember that like a redbud, you also need strong roots. And, like a redbud, your beauty will be revealed . . . in time.

Reaching Out

think of lovers as trees,
growing to and from one another
searching for the same light.
—WARSAN SHIRE

Looking for a better life? If so, here is the key: Reach out and make someone else's life a little better. Not just every once in a while, but as a regular and consistent action. Give to someone else, make their day a little brighter, and you will make a marvelous discovery. By bringing a little joy into someone else's life, you also make your life a little brighter, too.

Your acts of reaching out don't have to be grand or impressive. It's often the little things we do for others that make a difference. A vibrant "Thank you" to the clerk in the pharmacy who noted that the bottle of vitamins you were buying was part of a BOGO sale. A friendly greeting and comment about the weather to the barber cutting your hair. A cheerful conversation with the young man with Down syndrome at the hardware store helping you locate a special tool. Assisting a neighbor moving to a new location. Signaling a driver to cut in front of you as you wait for a traffic light to change. Hugging a former colleague you haven't seen in a while.

Reach out and touch someone's life. Every day.

My earliest years were spent in West Los Angeles. One of my favorite sensory memories were numerous gardenia trees scattered around the front yard of our house. Each of the trees sported a rounded crown of thick, glossy, leathery, dark-green leaves complemented with brilliant-white, showy flowers that bloomed from spring through early summer. The flowers most captured my attention. To this day I can recall their distinctive scent. The fragrance was intoxicating, even for a small lad who knew very little about the wonders of botany. Walking outside the front door was always an exhilarating experience with the brilliance of flowers and the delight of a most pungent aroma filling the atmosphere. Even some seven decades later and a residence 2,650 miles away from LA, that bouquet still lingers in my mind. I can scarcely walk by a gardenia tree in a nursery or arboretum without conjuring all sorts of pleasant memories. Their visual and olfactory appeals are without measure.

Gardenias give much pleasure to humans, pleasure without expectation of reciprocity.

While there are numerous rewards in helping other people—making their days and lives a little sunnier—there is a cautionary note to consider. When we reach out in expectation of a reward or a celebration of our good deeds, we defeat the overall purpose of those actions. We don't do good things for rewards that may come afterward. Doing good is its own reward. Knowing you have touched someone's life brings you peace and calmness in your own life. Requiring some sort of reciprocity in return defeats the very purpose.

A gardenia expects nothing in return for its color and fragrance. Much of its beauty is in the experiences it shares with others.

In Practice:

Mow your neighbor's lawn while they are away on vacation. Volunteer at your local food bank. If someone is unhappy, share one of your smiles. Offer to babysit your sibling's children so they can have a night out. Teach someone a new skill. Dust the bookcase or wash the dishes, even when it's not your turn. Allow someone to cut in line at the post office. Donate to a local charity. When a friend is sick, offer to pick up their groceries or medications. Pay for someone's coffee. Take your spouse or best friend to that new restaurant in town because—well, just because. Bottom line: There are a zillion ways to improve the lives of others. Every. Single. Day.

For Journaling:

Psychological research has proven that acts of generosity benefit not only recipients but also those who share themselves with others. Both individuals gain a sense of well-being and positive mental health. What often happens is that areas of our brain—particularly those associated with social connection and pleasure—are stimulated and activated. When done daily or regularly, generosity begets more generosity. We share love with others and with ourselves. You will discover positive stories and memorable anecdotes to add to your journal. Over time, you will accumulate a collection of positive affirmations to reread and celebrate.

Think About . . .

Do something nice for someone else, and don't tell anyone about it. Dawn redwood trees bring visual joy into our lives. They ask for nothing in return.

Carpe Diem

I want to do . . . what spring
does with cherry trees.
—PABLO NERUDA

Know that a day is neither good nor bad. Each day has a sunrise and a sunset. Each day is twenty-four hours long, representing one complete rotation of the Earth on its axis. A day is a day is a day. They are all the same, at least from a scientific standpoint. Most significant is not the goodness of that day; it is what we do with our day that influences our perception of it. Our attitude determines how good or bad the twenty-four-hour period seems.

Consider the acacia tree—a species prominent across the savannas and grasslands of Africa. With its classic umbrella-like canopy and arcing branches, acacias stand triumphant in an often-demanding environment. With its V-like structure, twisted trunk, and iconic spread, it is the epitome of beauty and grace—a botanical sentinel in an untamed land. Photos of this tree are often used in the opening credits of documentaries on Africa or on the covers of books about the wildlife of this enigmatic continent. This tree, and this tree alone, has come to symbolize the wonder of nature in sub-Saharan Africa.

But the acacia's leaves might be its most distinctive feature. Often feathery and small, they prevent the rapid evaporation of water in an arid environment. But they have also evolved to affect their longevity. You see, acacia leaves are a favorite food for giraffes. The height of an acacia tree is just right for these long-necked animals to browse among the leaves. However, as giraffes begin their feeding on one tree, the leaves release ethylene gas. This stimulates other acacias in the area to flood their leaves with unappetizing and unsavory tannins. In short, the attitude of one tree can affect the survival of other trees. One affects many.

Basic fact: The way you approach your day often determines how that day will turn out. Do you do so with spirit, determination, and love? Or do you begin a new day dreading a work assignment, fearing heavy traffic on the road, or detesting the bills you have to pay? The choice is yours. Ultimately the attitude and frame of mind you choose determines the degree of satisfaction derived from each day.

Good thoughts: good day.

In Practice:

Here's a ritual you may want to make part of your morning routine. Give yourself a few extra minutes for the drive to work. When you park your car, turn off the car engine, lean back, and prepare your mind for the day ahead. Instead of just rushing into work, close your eyes and create a vivid mental image of the day before you. Run this mental image through your mind, envisioning the tasks ahead, the people you will interact with, and the routines of the day. This five-minute preparation can help ensure that your day will be organized. It enables you to feel more composed and less stressed. By taking time to visualize, you can prepare your mind for the day's events and how you will approach them. Try it. You will be pleasantly surprised at the optimistic attitude generated. Better still, you will experience a more positive outlook on your day in tandem with a greater feeling of control.

For Journaling:

Consider the following quote from Henry David Thoreau: "To affect the quality of the day, that is the highest of arts." Now, think about the following two questions:

- In what ways do you affect the quality of *your* day?
- What do you do, regularly, to improve the quality of others' days?

Take some time to record your responses to those queries. Make that recording a regular, perhaps even daily, practice. In turn, you'll begin to notice some subtle changes in your attitude, perspective, and orientation. You'll see new opportunities for self-improvement as well as incentives to positively and actively affect the lives of others. Most important, you'll have an objective for the day, an incentive for positivity.

Think About . . .

Take five minutes and closely watch a flowering tree in the spring. How do you feel? Terrific! Okay, now make that your day.

Life: A Do-It-Yourself Project

For me, trees have always
been the most penetrating preachers.
I revere them when they live . . . in forests and groves.
And even more I revere them
when they stand alone.
—HERMAN HESSE

Several years ago, I had the pleasure of collaborating with a colleague on a series of professional workshops. She and I had been contracted to conduct a series of seminars in school districts throughout several southern states. The workshops focused on practices that would help teachers develop more dynamic classroom curricula, using some of the latest and most effective research.

My friend has a distinctive and positive outlook on the teaching profession and on life. She says, "Life is a do-it-yourself project." Her belief is that the best and most successful classrooms are places in which teachers continuously learn and grow with their students. So, too, does she believe that, as individuals, we are in charge of not only who we are but also who we can become.

Located just off 17-Mile Drive in Pebble Beach, California, is perhaps the most photographed tree in North America. Known as the Lone Cypress, it proudly stands atop a rocky headland overlooking Carmel Bay. This quintessential specimen hugs an ancient granite outcropping where it has survived ferocious and brutal storms, the persistent onslaught of salt spray, encroaching blankets of fog, a minimalist ecosystem that would extinguish other species, and at least one instance of criminal arson. The tree is believed to have germinated around 1750—a time when what is now California was a part of New Spain.

Over the decades, the wind and salt spray have forced changes in the tree's growth. Where it once had a lush dome-shaped canopy (as depicted in nineteenth-century photographs and illustrations), its current appearance is economical and sparse. So, too, has it adapted to its rocky existence by anchoring its roots in numerous places along the cliff. Consequently, over centuries, its entirety has endured the persistent onslaught of oceanic squalls, regular atmospheric disturbances, a challenging environment, and unfavorable human intervention.

It has survived by changing. As such, it is a totem among admirers.

We do ourselves a great disservice when we fail to take the time to realize our personal need for improvement or enhancement. Too often, we think that because we have a college degree or that we have been working in a specific field for *X* number of years, we have our act together. We know the procedures, rules, and expectations of our profession. We know what we have to do, and we get it done. But (and this is a big *but*) we often find ourselves in a mental rut because we have standardized our lives as much as we have standardized the requisites of our job.

We get far too comfortable being comfortable.

The good life is more than a complacency with what we have and what we've accomplished. It's also the realization we always have opportunities to improve and progress. It's about taking charge of our destiny, moving beyond any imperfections, and reaching for something more. It's not about accepting life as it is, but always about becoming just a little bit happier, a little bit wiser, a little bit better (or, like a certain cypress tree on the central coast of California, a little bit stronger). Perhaps the question we should ask ourselves is *Do I let life lead me, or am I in charge of my own living*?

Remember, *life is a do-it-yourself project.*

In Practice:

Here's a quote from George Bernard Shaw: "Life isn't about finding yourself. Life is about creating yourself." Take a moment and think about some of the things you have done in the past week that are personal reactions or attitudes. You might discover that a few items on that list related more to *enduring life* than with *creating life (Whew, I made it to the end of the week without losing my temper once)*. You may want to pause and consider some proactive ways in which you can grow and improve. Pick one of the following statements and make it your objective for the day.

- I can share more gratitude with my colleagues at work.
- I can take the time to attend my son's chess tournament.

- I can be more helpful in ensuring the cleanliness of our street.
- I can smile more, particularly at the folks I see in public.
- I can volunteer tutor at the literacy center.
- I can donate some unused kitchen items to a local charity.
- I can read to children at the local library.

For Journaling:

When we acknowledge the potential for growth in our lives, we celebrate the possibilities for self-improvement and self-development. People who resist change and say, "That's the way I've always done it," are stuck in a same-old, same-old universe. The implication is that if it worked in the past, it will surely work in the future. Coping with the world by clinging to the past makes life static, stagnant, and unrewarding. Instead, consider journaling about some of the ways you are changing, improving, or moving forward. What are you doing to become a better person? What are you discarding; what are you embracing? Focus your journaling on the positive (and regular) changes you are (or can be) making in your life, and you'll note some amazing things happening.

Think About . . .

Automobile logic: You can never move forward when you're constantly in park. Tree logic: You can never grow tall unless you constantly reach for the sunshine (human logic: same thing).

Ask Yourself How You're Doing

Trees are sanctuaries.
Whoever knows how to speak to them,
whoever knows how to listen to them,
can learn the truth.
—HERMAN HESSE

If you've ever had an MRI, you know they are noisy, confining, and somewhat uncomfortable. But they are also lifesavers. And, for that, we can thank Isidor Isaac Rabi. He was awarded the Nobel Prize in Physics in 1944 for his lifelong work on nuclear magnetic resonance—the basic foundation for MRIs.

After his acceptance speech for the Nobel Prize, Rabi was asked about some of the major influences in his life. He told the story about how he grew up in Brooklyn. When his friends all came home from school, their parents always asked them, "What did you learn in school today?" However, when Isidor came home from school each day, his mother always asked him, "Izzy, did you ask a good question today?" He shared how that single question from his mother every day helped him develop the inquisitive mind necessary for academic success and his eventual scientific discoveries.

It's also a query for ourselves.

Here's a question to ask yourself on a regular basis: *Hey [insert name], have I asked a good question about myself this week*? This self-examination offers you an opportunity to reflect on your internal growth and desire for improvement. It is also an opportunity for you to consider one of the most significant elements of self-awareness. The questions you ask yourself help determine how much you are growing as a loving and caring individual. Here are a few samples:

- In what ways did I compliment others?
- How have I expressed my love or admiration of others?
- How did I make someone's life a little better?
- What do I need to do to grow emotionally?
- What's really important in my life?
- How did I express my curiosity?
- How am I growing?
- What should be my goal for the coming week?

While this does not need to be a daily activity, it should be a regular activity—something planned and scheduled as a normal part of your week. A systematic self-reflection offers you a unique opportunity to assess where you are going and how you plan to get there. Truth be told, our internal growth and development do not result from a haphazard collection of strategies. Rather, they emerge from our faithful adherence to a planned series of goals that keeps us pointed in the right direction and on the right track.

Palm trees can be found in a wide variety of environments—from the arid deserts of the Middle East to the coastlines of South Pacific islands; from the forests of Colombia to the bustling streets of Miami Beach; from the backyards of Mediterranean estates to the unspoiled landscapes of Southeast Asia. All have different ecosystems and different challenges. As a result, the more than 2,600 species of palm trees have each developed a number of adaptations to survive in a specific location. Anthropomorphically speaking, they have self-assessed and adapted accordingly.

Palm trees have a prodigious and massive root system that quite often reaches depths of thirty feet or more. As a result, palms can survive in environments with limited rainfall or inadequate water resources. They also have wide leaves that allow them to capture lots of sunlight, thus improving their photosynthetic efficiency. In addition, palm trees can store vast quantities of water in their trunks, which allows them to survive long droughts or other periods when water is at a premium. This is particularly important in desert environments.

The questions we consciously ask ourselves give us opportunity to adapt to our own environments. If we ask, *How have I shown my appreciation for others this past week*? and self-respond, "Very little," then we have both reason and rationale to adjust our thinking and actions and make that a priority for the following week. Self-questioning also offers opportunity and incentive to alter our habits and provide necessary perspective. Instead of just thinking that we're doing good work, we can offer ourselves valid data upon which to act.

You will undoubtedly find this perspective refreshing and insightful. Now, instead of just plowing your way through life, you can regularly assess where you've been and where you still need to go. The result quite often is greater peace and comfort.

In Practice:

On Friday evening or Saturday morning, ask yourself one of the following two questions:

- "How did I make the world a better place this past week?"
- "How did I make myself a better person last week?"

Write a one-sentence response to your question. For example, you might say, "The world is a better place because I decided to volunteer at our local Salvation Army office." Or "I am a better person because I shared my artistic talents at the local community center." If you can't come up with a response to either question, you may want to take a little time and think about an equally positive (alternative) response ("I had way too many things on my to-do list to make the world a better place this week. Perhaps I should have prioritized my assignments so that I would have some available time for a contribution to the world"). By engaging in this activity on a regular basis—such as weekly—you will be able to set some realistic goals for more personal engagement as well as self-improvement.

For Journaling:

Here's a quote from influential psychiatrist and psychologist Carl Jung: "Who looks outside, dreams; who looks inside, awakes." What does that statement mean for you? How might those words shape the questions you could ask yourself? Here are some sample responses that might be appropriate for journaling:

- "When we look outside ourselves for answers we are only dealing with dreams. However, whenever I look inside myself for some self-improvement I begin to take action for those dreams."
- "I guess we spend way too much time imagining self-improvement rather than doing self-improvement. That is to say, self-improvement must be an active process generated from within a person. That's where it has the most influence."
- "Dreaming about a better life is okay. At least it gets me started. The reality of the situation is that self-improvement is a personal choice. I can become my true self when I take responsibility for my own growth and development."

What will you write?

Think About . . .

In ancient mythologies, trees are often regarded as sources of wisdom and erudition. The Japanese concept of kaizen—making small daily improvements—is demonstrated by the tiny bit of growth trees make every day. Truly a lesson for us all.

Active Listening

The forest is not only something to be understood,
it is also something to be felt.
—JOAN MALOOF

Have you ever had a conversation with someone and felt like the two of you were in a nonstop race to get your thoughts and opinions out with little regard for the other person's? You want to say your piece, make your stand, voice your thoughts as soon as the other person stops talking. The other person is doing the same thing. In the end, you both wind up talking, but neither one is listening.

Our egos tell us that we'd better get our position out there or the other person will ultimately "win" the conversation. As a result, conversations often involve each person waiting impatiently for the other to finish so that she/he can get their thoughts spoken. Conversations become races: Who can get their words in quickest, who can hold the floor the longest? Stress levels escalate, pressures to perform accelerate, and a mutual exchange of ideas deteriorates.

Biologically speaking, trees don't listen. But if you've ever had occasion to walk through a forest, any forest, you will quickly sense that they practice a unique form of listening. On various excursions through forests, Phyllis and I have made exclamations about the wonder of the trees; we have happily said, quite out loud, how marvelous these trees are, how impressive their stand against the elements, and how magnificent their extended lives along a slice of forested geography. Our words are celebrations upon the wind—out-loud exclamations about magnificent beings whose stature arouses both awe and admiration.

We are aware that the trees aren't listening in the way we do. But they do evidence a most peaceful response to us. Our statements are never interrupted; they are uttered without disruption or disturbance. They may float past these towering titans or linger on the wind, but a sudden retort is never forthcoming. We shower them with verbal respect, and they respond with arboreal silence, allowing the words to settle into the environment like soft snow in winter. There is no competition here, no interruptions or challenges. Words flow, language floats through long branches, and a peacefulness pervades.

Being an active listener is a conversation skill that can reap enormous benefits. Instead of trying to interject yourself and your ego into a conversation, focus instead on what another person is saying. Reflect on their words, and use those words in your responses. Instead of saying something like "Oh, I did the same thing, let me tell you about my experiences," or "Here's what I think," try some dedicated listening instead. You will surrender your need for attention and shine the light instead on someone else.

What you will notice is the other person's change in attitude. They will be considerably more relaxed, confident, and accepting because they know they are being listened to.

Or think about it this way: *listen* and *silent* are both spelled with the same six letters.

The ultimate benefit of active listening: You'll feel more relaxed knowing you don't have to make a point or argue a disagreement. You'll also be able to shine the light on another person, giving someone else the attention and you the inner peace and satisfaction that result from building others up rather than shouting them down. A side benefit is that your conversations with others will lessen your own anxiety and increase your mutual appreciation.

Just like a walk in the forest.

In Practice:

If you'd like to better understand something another person has said, you should ask for clarification. But don't focus so much on insignificant details that you miss the big picture they are trying to describe for you. Questions with more emphasis on emotions solicit better responses than those with an emphasis on details. Several psychologists have emphatically stated that when we weave questions into any conversation—particularly during a personal or emotional context—we are inviting deeper engagement in the discussion in addition to sparking reciprocal interest. So, too, are we demonstrating and building our emotional intelligence. Potential questions include

- "How do you feel about ________________?"
- "Would you ever want to ________________?"
- "Do you have any additional thoughts about ________________?"
- "What did you most enjoy about ________________?"

For Journaling:

After a conversation with someone, take a few moments and record your responses to the following statements. All are part of an emphasis on active listening:

- *I frequently told the other person what I heard.* (In any conversation, tell the other person what you understood ["Sounds like your trip to the Van Gogh Museum in Amsterdam was really exciting!"]. This ensures that you've captured accurately their thoughts, ideas, or emotions. It also helps the other person feel validated and recognized.)
- *I occasionally paraphrased what the other person said.* (Good listeners always paraphrase. For example, you might say, "In other words, you're frustrated," or "I'm hearing that you're confused about the impact of climate change." Summarize what you've heard and give the person the opportunity to say whether you've captured their meaning or intent.)
- *I was aware of some nonverbal cues.* (Good listeners also focus on body language, facial expressions, tone of voice, and speed of speech. How people speak to each other is just as important as what they say. Listening is improved with an attention to actions as well as verbiage.)

Think About . . .

We know that the trees within a forest constantly communicate with one another via an underground system of mycelium—a mass of branched, tubular filaments of fungi. On the other hand, we humans quite often spend too much of our time taking turns not listening to one another.

Time to Slow Down

We need hours of aimless wandering
or spates of time sitting on park benches,
observing the . . . canopy of treetops.
—MAYA ANGELOU

It was time to get away: a day for Phyllis to get away from the challenges of running a local art association, a day for me to get away from a writing schedule with several conflicting deadlines. Our agendas were packed with responsibilities and assignments that consumed massive amounts of time and equal amounts of energy. A day on long trails through a forest of white pines and eastern hemlocks was necessary for both spirit and soul.

While sauntering along a streamside trail, we talked about our overburdened schedules and packed days. Although retired, it seemed as though we just got busier and busier. Time to simply relax had been lost to self-inflicted duties and constant obligations. Then, as we approached a small rivulet, I saw a sprig of white pine just to my left.

It was solitary—a single young tree drinking in the sunlight and gripping the earth with fragile roots. Most noticeable was the realization that it was surviving quite well. It was peaceful, calm, and quite collected. It was not fighting fierce winds, the gnawing of hungry deer, or the indignity of someone's dog using it as a rest stop. It was merely basking in quietude, enjoying the day without a rush to do anything or go anywhere.

Recent research has given credence to a basic fact of life: Our lives are overcrowded and filled with far too many shoulds and musts. We attempt to multitask when scientists tell us that human brains are, from an evolutionary standpoint, insufficiently developed to juggle multiple projects and rampant responsibilities. We try to cram far too much into our lives and the lives of our children (soccer practice, art classes, piano lessons, and softball games anyone?). Our lives are dictated by clocks, watches, and calendars full of appointments. We rush through life.

It's time to slow down.

Staring at the young pine I was reminded that time in nature is time for inner peace, time for quality living. Our schedules become irrelevant and unnecessary. We are calmed and comforted in the natural world. Mental and physical easing are natural byproducts of time among tall timbers or across wide fields. Peacefulness abounds. Anxiety and inner struggles dissipate. Life is slowed, and minds are cleared. We regain our humanness. We return from this break mentally stronger, sharper, more creative, and certainly more focused. We are cleansed. And purified.

Ah, the wisdom of a young tree bathed in sunshine.

In Practice:

Convincing research shows that time spent among trees improves mental awareness, engenders positive attitudes, mitigates psychological stress, and fosters a greater enjoyment of life—but only if we take the time to listen. All too often, we walk through a forest looking but rarely listening. Listening gives us the opportunity to savor many elements within the forest without regard for time or schedules. This is time to pause, close our eyes, and absorb the sounds all around. In your journeys, listen for the whisper of leaves in the wind, the rubbing of branches, the chirping of birds, the scurry of tiny animals, the trickle of water, the piddle of raindrops, the cascade of a breeze, the dropping of seeds, a crescendo of thunder, the flap of wings, or simply the presence of quiet. Frequent pauses in your ventures through the forest can offer opportunity to hear the true sounds of life. You'll uncover some calmness and internal serenity in those hesitations.

For Journaling:

On your return from a forest walk, take time to record your listening experiences.

- What were some new sounds discovered?
- Which sounds were most pleasing?
- Which sounds would you like to hear again?
- Which sounds were musical; which were magical?
- In what ways did you leave the forest different from when you entered?
- How did an emphasis on listening improve your overall well-being?

Think About . . .

We live in a multitasking world—trying to cram as much as we can into twenty-four hours. On the other hand, many trees, such as the purple lily magnolia, the white cedar, and the Japanese snowbell tree, take a long time to reach their full heights.

Did you know that slow-growing trees, on average, live much longer than fast-growing trees? There's botanical evidence to show that the slower a tree grows, the more time it has to store nutrients and establish strong root systems. Hmmm.

365 Years from Now

I realize there's something
incredibly honest about trees in winter,
how they're experts at letting things go.
—JEFFREY MCDANIEL

When I was growing up, my father had a saying: "You know, 365 years from now, nobody's going to give a damn." For the longest time, I thought that was the most negative thing he ever said. I didn't get it. Yet as I continued my journey through high school, college, the U.S. Coast Guard, graduate school, my first teaching job, and eventually a career as a college professor, I slowly began to see the wisdom of his words.

What I didn't realize in my youth was that too often we tend to blow life's situations way out of proportion. We are worked up over small things, crowding our lives with far too many distractions and worries that, in reality, are inconsequential, yet we make them far larger than they really are. Then we have a life we have made full of unnecessary burdens that suck our energy and squash our spirit.

You tripped over a child's toy, someone made a right-hand turn from the left lane, you forgot where you put your glasses, you got lost on your way to a new furniture store, your favorite football team lost an important game, you had to wait in a long line at the bank, you had a disagreement with your spouse, you forgot to leave a tip for the server at your favorite restaurant, your car needs new brakes, or your four-year-old just said a bad word.

You know, 365 years from now, nobody's going to give a damn.

While those events may seem like major tragedies at the time, they are just irrelevant details in your everyday life. In the course of human events, they won't make any difference. But if we artificially give them more importance than they really deserve, we crowd our lives with all sorts of worries and stress. We create major problems where they don't exist.

During a camping trip in Cook Forest, a certified Old-Growth Forest in Pennsylvania and home to some of the tallest trees in the-northeastern United States, Phyllis and I took several hikes through an expanse of eastern hemlocks and ancient pines, some of which date back an estimated 350 years. Every so often we came across a tree that had lost a branch or two during a violent windstorm, another that had a mound of debris piled up at its base as the result of a spring flood, and a few that had been drilled into by several woodpeckers creating homes for their young. All the trees were still vibrant, all still reaching for the sky. I suspect that the broken branches or woodpecker holes were just minor irritations for these age-old timbers. They still continued their longevity in spite of the minor issues that befell them. Those problems were simply inconveniences, not disasters.

Earlier this morning, I wanted some scrambled eggs and toast for breakfast. After opening the refrigerator, I discovered we were out of eggs. I could have easily gone into a tantrum, stomped my feet in disgust, or beat myself up for not checking the refrigerator the previous day.

But then I remembered my father's words.

In Practice:

Instead of wasting your energy feeling angry and overwhelmed, look for calming strategies that offer an opportunity to step back and recompose yourself. Here are some most often recommended by experts:

- Count to 10, or 25, or 33.
- Take some deep breaths; slow down your respiration.
- Go for a short walk (around the block, around the office, through a shopping mall).
- Close your eyes, and slowly focus on the top of your head, then your forehead, your eyes, your nose, and so on down the length of your body.
- Listen to one of the playlists on your cell phone. Let your favorite music carry you into a different mood.
- Give yourself a time-out. Find a different place, a different chair, a different position. Change your environment, and you can change your mind.
- Record your emotions, feelings, or thoughts in your journal. What set you off? What calms you down?
- Close your eyes and imagine a stop sign. Create a picture of a stop sign in your mind, and allow yourself some time to pause.
- Look for ways to laugh: a humorous video on YouTube, a funny photo on Facebook or LinkedIn, an online joke, or a comedy on TV. Keep some funny books nearby, and read them every now and then.
- Write a short letter to yourself as to why you're angry. Then tear it up or delete it.

For Journaling:

Watch for the little events in your life—those that could potentially turn into major stressors. You may want to write down some of those daily situations to get a sense of just how many there are. Now, just imagine blowing up over each and every one. What a waste of time!

Think About . . .

People who try for perfection seldom have lives filled with inner peace. Note that there are no perfect trees, yet we love them still.

Your Greatest Accomplishment

He who plants a tree,
plants a hope.
—LUCY LARCOM

When people are asked about their greatest accomplishments in life, they are often prone to sharing external events. They cite graduation from a prestigious college, professional citations on their office wall, trophies in a display case at home, a photograph of themselves in the local paper, signing a contract with a well-respected institution, being able to fly first class as the result of a job promotion, or winning the conference championship in a particular sport.

For many, their most meaningful accomplishments are hung on a wall or displayed in an album.

But the life well lived is not one of accumulating awards or commendations from others but rather one of constant self-improvement from within. It's not so much about what we have won but more about what we have accomplished internally.

Almonds are one of the earliest domesticated fruits, first appearing in the Early Bronze Age. Native to Iran, approximately 80 percent of the world's almonds are now cultivated in California, where more than 1 million acres are devoted to almond trees.

Often classified as a nutritionally dense food for humans, almonds are packed with protein, riboflavin, niacin, vitamin E, calcium, copper, iron, magnesium, manganese, phosphorus, and zinc. They also contain substantial dietary fiber, oleic acid, and polyunsaturated fats. Almonds are rich in phytosterols—plant compounds that can lower cholesterol and reduce the risk of cancer. Almonds have a wide range of health benefits for humans that belie their size. In other words, their greatest accomplishments are internal rather than external.

Know that your internal development is much more important than your external accomplishments. So, too, you are judged not by what you have won in the past but rather by who you have become in the present. Your internal growth can often be gauged by your answers to the following:

- How have I made a difference in someone else's life?
- Am I willing to forgive others for their mistakes?
- Am I too stubborn, or am I more willing to consider the positions of other people?
- Can I see or understand another point of view?
- Can I remain calm and collected in an emergency?
- Have I brought some happiness or cheer into the lives of others?
- Am I willing to learn new things, or am I content with what I know now?
- Am I comfortable in seeking forgiveness?

What's really important in life: an accumulation of certificates and awards or an inner peace and contentment with who you are and what you can still become? The answer, as I'm sure you know, is in your heart, not your mind.

In Practice:

Here's something to consider at the end of each day: Provide the answer to either of the following two questions:

- How have I made myself a little better today?
- How have I made the lives of others a little better today?

You may not always come up with an answer, but, at the very least, you might come up with a focus for the following day.

For Journaling:

Imagine for a moment that you were asked to write the epitaph for your own tombstone. How would you want to be remembered? What would you most like to be known for? Take some time and record two or three possible epitaphs in your journal. Share them with a friend and ask for their thoughts. Which one do they like best? Over time, revise and edit those epitaphs until you arrive at one that clearly identifies you as an individual who made a difference in your own life or the lives of others. Now, be sure you live up to that statement. Here are a few epitaphs to get you started:

- No person is indispensable, but some are irreplaceable.
- A life well lived; she touched the world.
- He will be in the wind that moves by you.
- The song has ended, but the melody lingers on.

- She filled her life with goodness, then shared it with the world.
- The world is diminished by his absence but full of his presence.
- His wholeness became a part of us.
- She took in all the wonders of life and shared them unselfishly.

Think About . . .

Contemplate the Japanese practice of *ikigai*: Make your life meaningful by doing what you love, what you're good at, and what the world needs. A blossoming camillia tree does that all the time.

Understanding Others

If you have ever gone to the woods with me,
I must love you very much.
—MARY OLIVER

For many folks, their first encounter with the treelike saguaro cactus is less than auspicious. Here is a plant covered with sharp, penetrating spines that lives in an environment with a dearth of rainfall and an excess of high temperatures and exists with a very shallow root system. It is a plant that defies logic, one that violates what most gardeners east of the Rocky Mountains would want in their home gardens. It is sometimes characterized as strange, simply because it causes discomfort and irritation, it lives in a hostile ecosystem, and it provides shelter for a wide range of desert animals, a few with poisonous fangs. First-time visitors to the U.S. Southwest, more familiar with verdant forests of oak or long stretches of elm and hickory trees, may envision the saguaro as less a plant to admire and more one to ignore.

For many, saguaros are difficult to appreciate, difficult to love. They are, quite often, misunderstood.

That said, here's a strategy that will help you become a more peaceful and contented person: Spend more time trying to understand others rather than always trying to promote your own agenda. In other words, if you want to foster good relationships, good conversations, and good communication with others, take time to begin to understand them first rather than allowing your ego to take over and advocate for yourself. When we take time to first understand where other people are coming from, what is important in their lives, and their views about the world, we are extending an emotional hand. We are reaching out, establishing a positive encounter that nourishes the other person and provides a foundation for a fulfilling relationship.

Too often, we try to be understood before we try to understand others. We put ourselves first in any new encounter ("Here's what I've done, and here's what I'm going to do. Look at me"). On the other hand, when we inquire about others, we are demonstrating both respect and outreach. The conversation becomes less about two egos and more about what matters most: a healthy and effective form of communication. It's never about right and wrong; it's about building a relationship that celebrates the value of another person.

When you take time to understand a saguaro cactus you begin to develop a deep appreciation for this iconic desert dweller: (1) It can grow more than forty feet tall; (2) it can go for up to two years without rain; (3) 75 to 95 percent of its weight is water; (4) it doesn't begin to grow "arms" until it's about seventy years old; (5) it can live for up to two hundred years; (6) it can weigh as much as an African elephant (13,000 pounds); (7) most of its roots are only four to six inches deep; (8) a single cactus may capture up to two hundred gallons of water in a single rainfall; and (9) it will only grow one to one-and-a-half inches tall during its first eight years of life.

Seek to understand others first. Their lives will be enriched, and your spirit will be rejuvenated. Count on it.

In Practice:

To help us understand others better, experts offer several strategies we can easily incorporate into our everyday lives. Here are some opportunities:

- Listen closely to what people are saying.
- Try to see alternative points of view.
- Pay attention to the gestures and body language of others.
- Validate the emotions of other people.
- Offer your support and collaboration frequently but not obtrusively.
- Don't rely on assumptions. Inquire.
- Take an interest in the lives of other people.
- Open yourself up emotionally to connect with others.
- Be fully present in any conversation.

An excellent resource is *Emotional Intelligence: Why It Can Matter More Than I.Q.* (2005) by Daniel Goleman.

For Journaling:

The following are some sentence stems for your completion. At the end of each day, select one and record a response in your journal. Then make up a few of your own.

I listened closely to ________________ and learned that ________________.

I could sympathize with ________________ when she ________________.

I was able to see ________________'s point of view when he ________________.

I noticed that________________ communicates his feelings when he ________________.

I knew________________was upset when she ________________.

I wanted to offer my support when ________________.

At first, I thought she was wrong, but then I ________________.

I was really sad, and so I told him ________________.

I asked, and he told me that ________________.

I discovered that ________________ is really a very ________________.

Think About . . .

It's pretty easy being a critic, but it's more satisfying to be an admirer. For example, wisteria trees are often difficult to control, but they are also cited as some of the most beautiful trees in the world.

The Beauty Within

All our wisdom is stored in the trees.
—SANTOSH KALWAR

We wish we were perfect, but we also know that's not possible. Actually, perfection is more a desire than an achievement. Truth be told, we *all* have our imperfections, a few limitations, and most likely a few inadequacies. And you know what? That's okay.

While our respective features may differ, there is something similar we both must do. We must be willing to accept all those features as elements of our personality and our outlook on life. Yes, we're different, but we can learn to be more understanding of ourselves with an acknowledgment of our individual totality.

For example, you may find making new friends difficult. Perhaps you're shy or hesitant to reach out to others. That's okay. Instead of getting down on yourself, be more compassionate and accepting of who you are. You might say, *I'm not always comfortable in making friends, and that's okay. That's part of who I am.* Instead of focusing on one of your personality traits as a negative, accept it as part of your total being. Don't deny those feelings; just take them in stride. In so doing, you will become less frightened by them. They are only a small part of your being, not the totality of who you are.

Accept yourself as who you are: a composite of many traits instead of only a singular characteristic.

A few years back I took an extended journey through the Petrified Forest in northeastern Arizona. I was there to conduct some research for a book I was writing about long-living trees (*In Search of the Old Ones: An Odyssey among Ancient Trees*). My journeys through this vibrant geography revealed multicolored aggregations of stone and rock in myriad configurations. These were vestiges of coniferous trees—*Araucarioxylon arizonicum*—prehistoric giants that towered two hundred feet into Late Triassic skies (237 to 201.3 million years ago) in the northwestern corner of the supercontinent Pangaea.

These stony trees had been petrified through a process in which most, if not all, of their organic interiors had been replaced by mineral matter, typically quartz. Although their cellular structures have since disappeared, the shape and form of the trees was maintained. Over the millennia, a varied veneer of geological colors surfaced across their faces. Here was a mix of crimson, carmine, vermilion, amber, salmon, and peach deep within each stone's interior. The surfaces, too, gleamed with blotches of blond, ginger, and cerise. Each of these specimens was an artist's pallet overflowing with tints, pigments, and light. Each was different, each distinctive—their splendor magnified in the solar energy of a summer morning.

Each was beautiful in its own unique way.

Some of the rocks had interior cracks, missing chips, or a crusted layer of mud and dust. Like petrified trees, we also have a few imperfections here and there, and they certainly don't make us any less beautiful. In fact, when we are comfortable accepting the less-than-perfect parts of who we are, something interesting happens. We begin to notice the positive aspects of our life with a clearer focus and greater admiration. We see more of our true colors—those wonderful aspects of our lives that we celebrate and applaud. We become more comfortable with our entire being instead of perseverating on a few random negatives.

"I'm not perfect, but I'm comfortable with who I am, and I'm comfortable with who I can become" is a powerful statement: a commanding accolade for us all. The negative features are just a minor part of our whole being, not the entirety of our personality. Recognizing them as just a part of the bigger picture—not the whole picture—is an act of self-love, a way of acknowledging our humanity.

We admire a petrified tree for its splashes of color and its stony permanence. The tiny cracks and dusty exteriors are just slight imperfections in an otherwise magnificent wonder.

So, too, you.

In Practice:

A tree may have a missing leaf or two, a scarred section of bark, or a layer of moss clinging to its north side. Those elements don't detract from the overall spectacle of the tree. They are simply minor defects, tiny blemishes. The tree still stands tall and proud. What are two or three of your imperfections? Are they major obstacles in your growth or stature? Most likely not! Time to move on.

For Journaling:

Self-love includes saying positive things about yourself regularly, forgiving yourself when you make a mistake, accepting your imperfections, challenging yourself, recognizing your strengths, asking for help, making healthy choices, and being with people who understand and support you. How many of those traits do you practice on a regular basis? You may want to select one of those traits and describe it in your journal. For example,

- "I enjoy being with Marcie and Janice because they always see the good in me."
- "I think one of my personal strengths is my sense of humor. I always seem to make people smile whenever we're in a social situation."
- "I like me. I'm fun to be with, and I always see the best in others."
- "I'm always learning new things. I like keeping my mind active and engaged."
- "I'm a good parent because I always celebrate my kids and spend a lot of time with them."
- " I never forget to tell my parents how much I love them. That always makes me feel good. Them, too."

One of the things you'll notice about all those statements is that each one is phrased in the positive. Talk positively to yourself, and about yourself, and you lead a positive life.

Think About . . .

The Ladew Topiary Gardens in Monkton, Maryland, has trees in various shapes and configurations, each a visual spectacle! They're a good reminder that we shouldn't try to duplicate someone's else's life. Remember that you, too, are one of a kind!

On the Value of Persistence

I feel a great regard for trees;
they represent age and beauty and
the miracles of life and growth.
—LOUISE DICKINSON RICH

Early one fall, Phyllis and I journeyed to Pymatuning State Park near Jamestown, Pennsylvania, to spend a week camping amid a mélange of turning leaves, scampering critters, and zigzagging streams. During daylight hours, we hiked over rickety footbridges and along crooked trails that wandered through dense forests.

One day, less than a quarter mile below the earthen dam that impounds the 17,088-acre Pymatuning Reservoir, we found the oak. It was a striking titan—one that had been grasping the bank of the Shenango River for more than two hundred years (by our estimate). It was a tree whose constitution survived a devastating flood in 1913, endured generations of punishing winters, and stood rooted against all manner of environmental threats. It was supreme against the elements, mighty in the face of nature's challenges.

We were enthralled by its arboreal tenacity. Here was an organism that had weathered a plethora of trials and an abundance of life-threatening events. Yet for approximately two centuries, it was staunch against natural forces determined to topple it into the river. Throughout its life, it bent, it shook, and it most certainly swayed, but metaphorically speaking, it never lost sight of what it had to do to remain true to the heritage of oaks.

In our admiration of this tree, I was reminded of one of the signature dynamics of a satisfying life—persistence. The dictionary defines *persistence* as "the ability to go on resolutely or stubbornly in spite of opposition, importunity, or warning." While that definition defines many species of trees, it applies to our lives, too.

One of the barriers to a life of satisfaction and peace is that so many of us look for quick fixes—a technique or tip that might alter our perspective or change our direction if we just try it—once. If the strategy doesn't work the way we think it should, then we often move on to another strategy and another and another. We're on a constant search for instant perfection rather than a lifelong acceptance of change. The result is often frantic thinking, a draining of our emotions, and an increase in stress and frustration.

Consider that the best kind of change is that which occurs over a continuous period of time. Sustained commitment and unrelenting persistence are the keys to our ultimate success. We get to drink in the benefits and appreciate the dynamics of our renaissance. Our growth, our journey, is measured over months and years, and we get to enjoy the scenery along the way.

I have been fortunate to have met many individuals who are exemplars of persistence. They include a forty-six-year-old woman who came back to college to finish her degree and graduated summa cum laude, a young man who buried himself in auto mechanics and business courses so he could open his own auto repair shop, a former student who saved every nickel and dime so she could travel to Japan to visit her ninety-year-old grandmother one last time, a high school student who practiced kicking a soccer ball every day after school until the lights went off, and the business executive who wanted to run in the Boston Marathon and ran sixty miles every week for three years in preparation. Also, the individual reading this book who is seeking to make a better life for themselves via the wisdom of trees and lessons from the forest.

All embraced persistence. In spite of financial challenges, time constraints, family demands, emotional ups and downs, and occupational responsibilities, they set a long-term goal and pursued it with vigor and enthusiasm. All grew taller.

Like an oak.

In Practice:

I'm certain that one of your daily habits is brushing your teeth. It's easy to do and doesn't take much time. Your goals should be the same. Make self-improvement a regular habit, with an easy-to-accomplish process, a daily or regular activity. For example, say you want to improve your self-concept. You could write yourself a note (such as one of the following):

- I am an important person because I bring happiness to those I meet.
- I like myself because I'm getting a little better every day.
- I greet each day with a smile. Each person, too.
- I am trying to learn something new each day. I share what I learn with others.
- I think life is an amazing journey. So much to discover.

Easy to do and easy to insert into your busy day. Every so often, reread your notes and tell yourself that you are well on the way to self-improvement.

For Journaling:

Psychologists advise that a long-term focus on emotional goals is much more satisfying than a focus on material gains, such as working overtime in order to afford that flashy new car. The best improvement in our lives comes from within, not outside. Consider an affective goal, perhaps a new one each week or each month:

- I would like to be more patient in my conversations with others.
- I want to think more positively about who I am.
- I would like people to like me for who I am becoming.
- I believe in myself and what I can accomplish.
- I want to live life to its fullest. I want to enjoy every moment.

Write a selected goal in your journal. Consider posting it on your bathroom mirror, car dashboard, or cell phone. Refer to it often.

Think About . . .

In the Anton Valley of Panama is a most unusual forest. The cottonwood trees in this valley all have square trunks (four right angles). Even the rings of these trees grow in a square shape. You, too, may be different from everyone else. That doesn't mean you can't be amazing as well.

Pay It Forward

The true meaning of life is to plant trees
under whose shade you do not expect to sit.
—NELSON HENDERSON

It was my final semester—the last semester I was to teach before I retired. Along with three other courses, I taught a section of Introduction to American Education—a required course for preservice teachers and a free elective for all other majors. This particular class was composed of a diverse assembly of nursing students, computer science majors, history majors, journalism students, along with majors in biology, chemistry, sports management, and, of course, education. We were an eclectic assembly.

I worked hard to establish a community of learners—a self-supportive clan built on respect and celebration. I learned students' names quickly, tapped into their hobbies and interests, embraced different points of view, and constantly rewarded them with smiles and attention. There was a vibrancy in the air, and rare was the time when students were absent. New friendships were established, and common goals were pursued. We became less a class and more a village.

We also became a forest.

I define a forest as a group of trees that support one another (via the tangle of roots), interact with one another (via their underground mycelium), and collectively share sunshine and rain. A forest is a community of beings that grow together, share resources, and enrich the lives of every single member. There is a common spirit, an amalgam of biological intent and a collection of individuals living in harmony with one another.

I've long believed that college courses are quite similar to vibrant forests. Each individual begins the semester as a single entity in a brand-new environment. In time, given the right growing conditions, those individuals begin a most distinctive process. They begin to share common goals and contribute to the common good. They grow in harmony; they sustain one another. They become a vibrant community—less an assembly of individuals and more like a forest.

But college courses, just like forests, eventually come to an end, so I considered how this course might conclude. Was there some sort of celebration I could use or a final activity that would help everyone understand that learning is much less the memorization of facts, and more a potent form of communication and connection that celebrates the participation of all? I pondered for long hours.

Then, one day, while strolling down the hall outside my office, I overheard a brief discussion about the concept of paying it forward. Suddenly, an enormous light bulb flashed over my head. That was it! That was exactly what I needed to conclude the course and send students into their summer vacations with the true meaning of education.

So I stopped by my credit union and obtained twenty-four silver dollar coins. Placing them in my pocket, I walked into the last and final class. I began by telling students how much they had contributed to the class—individually and collectively. I then informed everyone that I would walk down every row and present each of them with a silver dollar and an invitation to pay it forward—sharing the basic objectives of the course with others. For example, I'd say, "Perhaps your local Little League team is short on funds. Donate your silver dollar so that they might be able to purchase an extra baseball. Or donate your silver dollar to your local public library so that they might be able to add one new book to their collection. Or perhaps your roommate is really short on cash at this point in the semester. Buy them a package of ramen noodles so they can make it through final exams." The decision was theirs; they didn't have to report back to me or write a paper. They were simply invited to pay it forward.

Then I walked up to each student's desk and, face-to-face, celebrated their individual performance and contributions to the class. For example, "Devon, I would like to thank you for all your energetic discussions in class. You really added much to our conversations. Your ideas are much appreciated." Or "Samantha, your papers were always full of passion and involvement. Thank you so much for the time and energy you put into your work. They were really a joy to read." Or "Walt, I was so excited to hear that you decided to switch your major to education. I think a new generation of kids will be the ultimate benefactors of your love of history. Thanks so much!"

After every short conversation I handed each student a silver dollar and shook their hand. Students reciprocated with an enormous smile, a most gracious "thank you," or an extended handshake. Three students hugged me, and one young lady even gave me a peck on the cheek (a first). A shy student, quite overcome with emotion (and a few tears), told me that no teacher or instructor had ever thanked her before. Another student insisted on a photograph with me—something he wanted to share with his parents. The final part of that class took about fifteen to twenty minutes but was clearly emotional and poignant. All were touched.

As the class slowly filed out the classroom, one individual gathered up his belongings and sauntered out to the parking lot and climbed into his car. As he rolled out the back gate, there was an enormous smile on his face—one that lasted throughout the entire thirty-minute drive home.

In Practice:

Know there is something magical about doing something thoughtful for others. That's particularly true when we make it a daily practice rather than something done occasionally or intermittently. Knowing you have the ability to make someone's day just a little better is a reward in itself. You always feel good when you give to others. Their day is better, and so is yours. Win-win.

You can pay it forward in a myriad of ways. If you need a few to get you started, consider the following:

- Pay for someone's coffee.
- Leave a note of encouragement in a library book.
- Plant a tree.
- Pick up litter on your afternoon walk.
- Donate used clothes.
- Walk your neighbor's dog.
- Write thank-you notes to colleagues.
- Ask for donations instead of gifts.

- Leave a good book behind.
- Donate blood.
- Put coupons on community boards.
- Do pro bono work for a community organization.
- Sponsor a child.

For Journaling:

Consider this quote from the Dalai Lama: "If you want others to be happy, practice compassion. If you want to be happy, practice compassion." What do those words mean to you? How could you incorporate those words into your daily activities? Record the responses to those questions in your journal and review them every so often. Consider how you could pay it forward for others.

Think About . . .

Banyan trees produce aerial roots that grow downward from their branches. When the roots reach the ground, they often take root and become woody trunks. These trees give us pause to contemplate the need to spread happiness and how that action keeps us well rooted.

Conclusion

When we walk into a grove of trees . . .
the magic of nature takes over and
the heaviness of life lifts a little.
—NATASSIA CASSINERO

One summer while traveling around myriad lochs of western Scotland, Phyllis and I came upon the Ardkinglas Estate just outside the tiny village of Cairndow (about one hour northwest of Glasgow). A luxuriant forest reminiscent of the *Lord of the Rings* movies, it was gilded, abundant, and verdant. Ferns waving in the breeze, moist trails looping beneath overhanging branches, a profusion of aged beeches, deciduous azaleas, late-flowering hydrangeas, enormous rhododendrons, towering mountain ashes, an ancient stone weir thrown across a meandering stream, and a ruined mill succumbing to a blanket of vegetation—all in a lively botanical expanse perfumed with splendid flowers and musty old logs. The day was dripping with humidity, and the atmosphere was rich with the anticipation of another afternoon rain shower.

Just off the puddled trail, we rested at a well-weathered gazebo tucked into the forest. Inside was a panoply of small wooden plaques—each etched with a poem, a verse, or a philosophical statement about the influence of nature or the wonder of trees. The brochure obtained at the start of the trail referred to this site of contemplation as a "scriptorium"—an enclave highlighting the thoughts and introspections of naturalistic philosophers—in this case, sages as diverse as St. Bernard ("You will find something more in woods than in books. Trees and stones will teach you that which you can never learn from masters"), Voltaire ("Nature has always had more force than education"), William Blake ("the green woods laugh with the voice of joy"), and John Muir ("In every walk with nature one receives far more than he seeks"). When found in gardens, scriptoriums are shrines of botanical celebration that laud the influence of nature.

My lifelong migration through the biological magnificence of forests, both near and far, has been through similar scriptoriums—nature's celebration of life permanently etched into the rough-hewn bark of thousands of sun-tipped guardians hugging long alpine territories, sheltering riverine valleys, or silhouetting dazzling summer sunsets. They are influential in their spread and provocative in their wisdom. In turn, each venture brought me closer to environmental truths. It has been an education traced by dusty footsteps and a constant passion for discovery. These are great pauses in the mandates of everyday life—ecological sanctuaries offering time for contemplation and consideration, respites and reflections.

I believe that scholarship is not confined to the sterility of technology-infused lecture halls, the dispassion of textbooks, or a reliance on googling. I have long been convinced that impressionable learning is a shared experience—a mutual connection of curiosity and intent. For me, this arboreal journey was a contact and contract with the forest, a (re)connection with biological imperatives. The best of scholarship.

When this expedition commenced, I was in search of answers; instead, I found truths. I discovered a realm of knowledge that is invisible yet now deeply ingrained in my fiber. I commanded myself to observe, to absorb, to soak, to embrace. The trees I visited and the forests I roamed were mentors beyond knowledge; they were environments of understanding and wide expanses of intellectual fulfillment. I was wrapped in their lives. I stood, disconnected from tight schedules, mandated appointments, and the clamor of mindless media. And in that standing I evolved.

The wisdom of trees is, I learned, engaging—and in perpetuity, embracing.

This writing has been a journey along an endless continuum—a sliver of visitation and contemplation. Though now in my golden years, I am ever the student. I am plugging holes and filling gaps unconsidered in my youth. Like the twining stem of a morning glory plant, I am wrapping myself around empty spaces and reaching out to unseen vistas. I continue to grow—knowing that learning is never static but eternally pulsing with investigative possibilities. My teachers now—quite often tall and silent—share their wisdom, impart their grace, and bestow their spirit as wise counselors upon the land.

Dear reader, this is not the end of a book. Rather, it is a contemplation of new possibilities, a consideration of fresh beginnings —a rebirth, a revival, and a personal restoration. In truth, it is a revitalization of our humanity, our possibilities. I'd like to imagine it as a celebration of a continuous journey toward personal satisfaction and lifelong happiness. Perhaps, with a keen concentration on the trees around us and the lessons in their lives, we can see more clearly . . . moving ever forward.

The forests await. Endeavor to pay attention.

You, too, will change.

In forests there is great wisdom.
Venture through.
Observe closely.
Learn much.
Grow!

Suggested Readings

Here are some of my favorite books—each with additional insights and counsel on living the good life. Consider them as positive additions to your personal library or reading list.

Beresford-Kroeger, Diana. *To Speak for the Trees: My Life's Journey from Ancient Celtic Wisdom to a Healing Vision of the Forest.* Portland, OR: Timber Press, 2019.

Breathnach, Sarah Ban. *Simple Abundance: 365 Days to a Balanced and Joyful Life.* New York: Grand Central Publishing, 2019.

Brown, Brené. *Dare to Lead: Brave Work. Tough Conversations. Whole Hearts.* New York: Random House, 2018.

Carlson, Richard. *Stop Thinking, Start Living.* New York: HarperCollins, 1997.

Chopra, Deepak. *The Seven Spiritual Laws of Success.* New York: Amber-Allen Publishing, 2015.

Clear, James. *Atomic Habits: An Easy & Proven Way to Build Good Habits & Break Bad Ones.* New York: Avery, 2018.

Covey, Stephen. *The 7 Habits of Highly Effective People.* New York: Simon & Schuster, 2020.

Duckworth, Angela. *Grit: The Power of Passion and Perseverance.* New York: Scribner, 2018.

Fredericks, Anthony D. *From Fizzle to Sizzle: The Hidden Forces Crushing Your Creativity and How You Can Overcome Them.* Indianapolis, IN: Blue River Books, 2022.

Fulghum, Robert. *All I Really Need to Know I Learned in Kindergarten.* New York, Ballentine Books, 2003.

Goggins, David. *Can't Hurt Me: Master Your Mind and Defy the Odds.* Austin, TX: Lioncrest Publishing, 2018.

Goleman, Daniel. *Emotional Intelligence: Why It Can Matter More Than I.Q.* New York: Bantam, 2005.

Green, David. *The Laws of Human Nature.* New York: Penguin, 2019.

Iyer, Pico. *The Art of Stillness.* New York: Simon & Schuster, 2014.

Keltner, Dacher. *Awe: The New Science of Everyday Wonder and How It Can Transform Your Life.* New York: Penguin, 2024.

Lightman, Alan. *In Praise of Wasting Time.* New York: Simon & Schuster, 2018.

Maxwell, John C. *Failing Forward: Turning Mistakes into Stepping Stones for Success.* New York: HarperCollins, 2007.

McRaven, William. *Make Your Bed: Little Things That Can Change Your Life . . . and Maybe the World.* New York: Grand Central Publishing, 2017.

Neff, Kristin. *Self-Compassion: The Proven Power of Being Kind to Yourself.* New York: HarperCollins, 2015.

Richardson, Cheryl. *Take Time for Your Life: A Personal Coach's 7-Step Program for Creating the Life You Want.* New York: Harmony, 1999.

Schwartz, David. *The Magic of Thinking Big.* New York: Magdalene Press, 2015.

Spiegel, Cyndie. *A Year of Positive Thinking: Daily Inspiration, Wisdom, and Courage*. Emeryville, CA: Althea Press, 2018.

Tolle, Eckhard. *The Power of Now: A Guide to Spiritual Enlightenment*. New York: New World Library, 2004.

Williams, Mark, and Danny Penman. *Mindfulness: An Eight-Week Plan for Finding Peace in a Frantic World*. New York: Rodale, 2011.

Acknowledgments

I am now within sight of my ninth decade. Although my pace has slowed over the years, I am ever mindful of one of life's great truths: There is wisdom in nature and comfort in its embrace. My lifelong journeys through vast forests, my presence among magnificent and towering timbers, and my transits along winding trails far beyond the cacophony of everyday life have given me an education unavailable in textbooks or cavernous lecture halls. Those treks have opened my eyes to an ancestral knowledge and communion with organisms that have existed on this planet long before the arrival of *Homo sapiens*.

In our transits through forests, we give ourselves a most wonderous gift: timeless lessons of renewal, tranquility, and joy. In the woods we have opportunity to discover our true selves, occasions to renew our spirit and refresh our humanity, instances to reconnect with others, and celebrations of life in both present and future days. We only need to stop and observe, pause and reflect. And in so doing, we grow ever upward.

Just like the trees.

So, too, do wooded acres give us one of life's most important lessons: that of connections. For, just as trees grow best in the company of their own, so do we.

Trees show us the importance of networks—the intermingling of roots, the sharing of vital nutrients and life-giving water, the persistent protection of a thick canopy, and the sturdiness of trunks during fierce storms. A forest is a vibrant association of individuals who support one another so that all may survive, so that all may prosper. A "mutual admiration society" if you will.

In many ways, a book—this book—is also a forest. The pages you have read exist, not just because of a single person (the author), but also because of the contributions of many individuals who gave it life, sustenance, and vitality far beyond its words. For that, I am forever grateful and sincerely appreciative.

Like a majestic stand of redwood trees, my immediate family provided constant support and sustenance throughout this journey. My wife, Phyllis, whom you met in several of these essays, journeyed with me to many of the trees and forests profiled in these pages. From Florida to California, Colorado to Maine, and North Carolina to Utah, her perceptions and introspections about species and groves were instrumental in developing the thesis for many essays. She is my greatest supporter, my constant muse. Our daughter, Rebecca, a most talented artist living in northern England, contributed the painting on the cover of the book. Her vision of trees as icons of growth and renewal permeates all her work. Our son, Jonathan, saved his father from embarrassment and frustration in solving a word processing conundrum that was making random sections of the edited manuscript disappear into the far reaches of cyberspace. To them, my forever love.

I am especially indebted to my editor, Darcie Abbene, for her insightful and passionate guidance, her eye for specific details and clear explanation, along with her resolute support of this project throughout its creation and development. Her engagement in this book is a professional honor and a celebration of editorial wisdom unparalleled in the world of publishing. She stands as a totem of excellence among peers; a beacon of admiration, respect, and regard. How fortunate I was to have her counsel and influence throughout this two-year endeavor.

So, too, am I thankful for Larissa Henoch, the art director for HCI Books, whose clear design and editorial layout transformed words and sentences into rich arrays of substance and intent. Her professional expertise is reflected throughout the entirety of these pages. The copyeditor, Bob Land, went through these essays with the proverbial fine-toothed comb. His sage suggestions for readability and improvement are most appreciated and most commended.

My dear friend, Beverly Read, infused her positivity and experience into several of these essays. Her keen eye for poetic detail, her embrace of the "good life," and her eagerness to tender advice and direction gave me much to ponder, and much to savor during the composition of words and concepts. So, too, her embrace of the book's subtitle was invaluable in shaping these thoughts.

Every other month or so, I have the pleasure of enjoying a tall pile of pancakes or a masterful three-egg omelet, along with endless cups of coffee, at a local restaurant with three former colleagues: Mike McGough, Pete Piepmeier, and Bob Lindsay. Informally, we are the ROMEOs (Retired Old Men Eating Out); more formally they are my sounding board, my fearsome critics, and my staunchest supporters. They embody so many of these essays in both word and deed—an ensemble of kindred souls and forever friends.

This book would not have evolved were it not for the ever-present encouragement, cheer, and affirmation of our dear friends and joyful traveling companions—Jack and Linda Sommer. Their great humor and endearing camaraderie are a tonic and a comfort for every creative pursuit. They truly embody, and share, the wisdom of this tome.

Like a grove of tall timbers—each sustaining the other—so, too, does an author have a "forest" of supporters who bring their suggestions, guidance, and passion to any literary endeavor. There are revelations in their outreach; foundation in their roots. To them all, as with the trees, I give fond thanks.

About the Author

Anthony D. Fredericks is a husband, father, grandfather, brother, uncle, and cousin. So, too, is he professor emeritus of education at York College of Pennsylvania where he taught science, creative writing, and teacher education courses for thirty years. He is a prolific and award-winning author of more than 180 books, including adult nonfiction (*In Search of the Old Ones*; *The Secret Life of Clams*), children's books (*Tall Tall Tree*; *Under One Rock*), and education titles (*Ace Your Teacher Interview*; *The Adjunct Professor's Complete Guide to Teaching College*). He has also written for an eclectic array of magazines and online journals including *High Country News*, *Hawai'i Magazine*, *Harrisburg Magazine*, *Teaching K-8*, *Writer's Journal*, *CNBC-Make It*, and *Psychology Today*, among others. A professional educator for more than a half century, he has presented science workshops, conducted natural history presentations, and made numerous keynote addresses throughout North America. He and his wife, Phyllis, live in York, Pennsylvania. For further information: www.anthonydfredericks.com.